Ahmad al-Mansur

Outside the Saʻdian tombs. Courtesy of Richard Smith.

Richard L. Smith

Ferrum College

Ahmad al-Mansur

Islamic Visionary

The Library of World Biography

Series Editor: Peter N. Stearns

PEARSON

Longman

New York   Boston   San Francisco
London   Toronto   Sydney   Tokyo   Singapore   Madrid
Mexico City   Munich   Paris   Cape Town   Hong Kong   Montreal

Executive Editor: Janet Lanphier
Executive/Senior/Marketing Manager: Sue Westmoreland
Production Manager: Virginia Riker
Senior Cover Design Manager: Nancy Danahy
Cover Photo: Mary Evans Picture Library
Senior Manufacturing Manager: Mary Fischer
Electronic Page Makeup: Alison Barth Burgoyne
Printer and Binder: RR Donnelley Harrisonburg
Cover Printer: Coral Graphics Services, Inc.

Library of Congress Cataloging-in-Publication Data

Smith, Richard L. (Richard Lee), 1945–
    Ahmad al-Mansur : Islamic visionary / Richard L. Smith.
        p. cm. — (The Library of world biography)
    Includes bibliographical references and index.
    ISBN 0-321-25044-3 (alk. paper)
        1. Morocco—History—1516–1830. 2. Ahl mad al-Manslār,
Sultan of Morocco, 1549–1603. 3. Islam—Africa, North. I. Title.
II. Series.

DT322.S65 2005
964'.025'092—dc22   2005020037

Please visit our website at www.ablongman.com

ISBN 0-321-25044-3

1 2 3 4 5 6 7 8 9 10—DOH—08 07 06 05

For my Mother and Father,
Virginia Lee Mounts Smith
and
Leon R. Smith, Jr.
Who imbued in me a love of learning

Contents

Editor's Preface

"Biography is history seen through the prism of a person."

—Louis Fischer

It is often challenging to identify the roles and experiences of individuals in world history. Larger forces predominate. Yet biography provides important access to world history. It shows how individuals helped shape the society around them. Biography also offers concrete illustrations of larger patterns in political and intellectual life, in family life, and in the economy.

The Longman Library of World Biography series seeks to capture the individuality and drama that mark human character. It deals with individuals operating in one of the main periods of world history, while also reflecting issues in the particular society around them. Here, the individual illustrates larger themes of time and place. The interplay between the personal and the general is always the key to using biography in history, and world history is no exception. Always, too, there is the question of personal agency: how much do individuals, even great ones, shape their own lives and environment, and how much are they shaped by the world around them?

Peter N. Stearns

Author's Preface

The sixteenth century was a transitional period during which not just states but whole civilizations seemed to cross each other on their paths of development. Western Europe, the Islamic world, and the interior of West Africa were then in crucial periods of change, each headed in its own direction but pausing in the presence of the other two. Standing at the junction of this passage was the Sultan of Morocco, Ahmad al-Mansur.

When students consider the sixteenth century, Ahmad al-Mansur (1549–1603) probably does not come to mind. History sometimes discovers individuals who went unnoticed in their own time yet whose significance takes on importance in retrospect. Other individuals are quite the opposite; their contemporaries may have considered them as movers and shakers, but their legacies don't comfortably fit into the constructs historians build for understanding the past. Often they are left out, sometimes unfairly. History does not always give its subjects their due.

Ahmad al-Mansur lived in an era of strong personalities, Queen Elizabeth of England, Philip II of Spain, and Sulayman the Magnificent being the most notable. A large cast of lesser known characters entered and exited his life: Dom Sebastian of Portugal, the last crusader king; Judar Pasha and Mahmud b. Zarqun, renegade commanders who conquered an empire in the heart of West Africa; and Bukar Lanbaru, spy extraordinaire, whose dirty tricks overthrew a dynasty, were the most notorious. Among his contemporaries, al-Mansur commanded attention. His influence and the impact of his actions extended far beyond Morocco, into the Mediterranean, through northwestern Europe, and across the Sahara into the valley of the Niger.

The sixteenth century was a period of nation building, and within the boundaries of Morocco al-Mansur created a powerful state structure. He was also a state destroyer who sent armies across the Sahara to conquer and plunder, leaving a legacy of ruin in the interior of West Africa. Morocco was at the far end of western Islam, the last bastion of the faith, and al-Mansur's role in his society depended as much on his religious position as on his political position. He claimed the holiest of roles, yet for many observers he could have been the prince whom Machiavelli used as his model for realpolitik, had al-Mansur only lived a century earlier. He was an extraordinary person: clever, charming, enterprising, pious, greedy, rapacious, and visionary. If his vision of a unified Islamic world did not materialize, the more practical consequences of his actions in building a centralized state—from what had been little more than a tribal confederation a century earlier—anticipated political developments in the impending modern era. For the student, he provides an insight into one of history's most vexing questions: How much impact can an individual have on his time? For the general reader, al-Mansur's story is a fascinating one that straddles historical periods and continents, empires and religions.

If Ahmad al-Mansur is one of the more overlooked characters in world history, his country also tends to be undernoticed. In the late sixteenth century Morocco was a place of note. Spain, England, and the Ottoman Empire courted, threatened, and worried about the government in Marrakesh—a tribute to al-Mansur's skill in both statecraft and public relations. But he was not all bluff. The armies of Morocco were large and well equipped with the latest gunpowder weapons. In foreign trade, Morocco was a leader in supplying two of the most valuable products fueling the emergent Atlantic economy, sugar and gold. By 1600 Morocco seemed poised to enter into the new world system then taking shape, much as Japan would do three centuries later. If all of this vanished as though by the wave of a wand, that hardly makes it unworthy of study, unless we truly believe that only the victors write the histories. In real history, not all stories have happy endings.

Biography is a crucial element of history. History is more than the interplay of important individuals, but to leave them out is to delete the human from the story of humanity. Yet the biographer must be careful: biography separated from history risks becoming a story without a point. In a study of anyone's life, certain characteristics will predominate, certain themes will emerge. Ahmad al-Mansur was absolutely convinced he had been sent on a divine mission. His preoccupation with this conviction appeared as a driving ambition characterized by persistence, focus, energy, and ruthlessness.

In exploring themes, the biographer must be careful not to use a subject as the embodiment of some ideal. Only a few people in history really were paragons of virtue, and perhaps a few more qualify as manifestations of evil: as a general rule, nice guys don't found empires. But the majority of those who end up in history books are almost always some mixture of good and bad, virtue and fallibility, idea and action, success and failure. They reflect the complexity of the human experience. They are not required by history to be ennobled or demonized. They are who they were.

Ahmad al-Mansur lived in a world that will be unfamiliar to most students today. If Marrakesh and Fez seem strange, Timbuktu and Gao, Tuwat and Taghaza will appear even more so. Hence this book must be not only a biography and a political history but a cultural, social, and economic history as well.

In writing about sixteenth-century Morocco and the West African interior, the historian has little more to depend on than the descriptions provided by contemporaries or those who lived later but had access to contemporary documents now lost. These sources deal with matters that are necessarily subjective, such as a person's character or motives, as well as those of a more concrete nature, such as the date of an event or the size of an army. Rarely do all the sources concur even on concrete information, and trying to piece together what really happened can be both exhilarating and frustrating. The student can see firsthand how historians must appraise such sources in order to determine which is more likely to be accurate (usually by a process of elimination), in many instances only to conclude that there is no definitive way of telling. Thus, the sources become a part of the narrative, inviting the reader to interact with the text.

The figure on the cover requires some explanation. In this series of biographies, images of the subjects usually appear on the cover and on the frontispiece. In many Islamic societies, however, the depiction of the human form has often been avoided even though it is not expressly forbidden in the Qur'an. Most Muslim rulers, including the Sa'dis, did not keep portrait painters and sculptors at court. As a result, no representation that has been definitively identified as Ahmad al-Mansur is available. A few possibilities do exist. One by the German artist Tobias Stimmer (1539–1584) is a painting on a wooden panel identified as "Muleamethes" (Mawlay Ahmad; Mawlay is a title), "Great King of Mauritania" (Morocco). Unfortunately, on further examination, this work is likely to have been done three years before Ahmad became sultan, with the legend added later.

A more likely candidate appears on the cover of this book and is from an engraving by the French cosmographer, Andre Thevet (c. 1516–1594). The image is taken from a book published in 1584 and is identified only as "Cherif, King of Fez and Morocco" (cherif, or sharif, refers to a descendant of the Prophet Muhammad). Thevet was widely traveled and is reputed to have visited the Ottoman Empire and "Barbarie," a general European term for North Africa. A caveat, however, may be in order. Thevet has been criticized recently by scholars as a plagiarist, poser, and fabricator of at least some of his travels.

On the transliteration of Arabic and, occasionally, Turkish, Berber, and Songhay words, standard usage is followed herein except for a few terms that have passed into modern English usage, as, for example, marabout (rather than the more technically correct murabit), caliph (rather than khalifa), casbah (rather than qasba), and Ottoman (rather than Osmanli). Only the diacritical marks ' and ' are used.

Acknowledgements

From the beginning of this project, my wife, Kathleen Charpentier Smith, has been my partner along every step of the way. My debt of gratitude to her is immeasurable. I would like to thank the Appalachian College Association for the award of a John B. Stephenson Fellowship, which provided the time and support to do much of the research on this book, and particularly Professor Andrew Baskin of Berea College. Many professionals in a number of libraries have offered valuable assistance to me; in particular, I am grateful to Cheryl Hundley and George Loveland of Stanley Library at Ferrum College and Ronald Smith, formerly of Butler Library at Columbia University. Professor Lloyd Cannaday and Brenda Sigmon of Patrick Henry Community College were especially helpful in the design of the maps. I also wish to acknowledge the administration of Ferrum College for its support through professional development grants, a timely sabbatical, and occasional release time. I appreciate the suggestions, advice, and criticisms of the following scholars who served as reviewers for the manuscript: Chris Bierwith, Murray State University; Patricia Gloster-Coates, Pace University; James A. Jones, West Chester University; Melvin E. Page, East Tennessee State University; Denis Paz, University of North Texas; and David Ulbrich, Ball State University. To my mentor and lifelong friend, Peter N. Stearns, I say thank you for teaching me so long ago how to do this kind of thing.

RICHARD L. SMITH

Ahmad al-Mansur

The Rise of the Sa'di Dynasty

Abu l'Abbas Ahmad, known to history by the titles al-Mansur, "the Victorious," and al-Dhahabi, "the Golden," became Sultan of Morocco on August 4, 1578, following a battle in which his brother, Abd al-Malik, the reigning sultan, and his nephew, Muhammad al-Mutawakkil, the former sultan, both died. A third king, the ruler of Portugal, died as well, prompting historians to dub this the Battle of the Three Kings. In Europe it was called the Battle of Alcazar, a corruption of the nearby town of Qasr al-Kabir, but in Morocco it was the Battle of Wadi al-Makhazin, after the river on the banks of which the struggle had raged.

War is one of those human activities that does not require consenting parties. If one party to a dispute decides to resort to war, the other must oblige or face destruction. Although war generally involves large numbers of men in an activity that determines their very existence, the decision to go to war has too often been made by a single individual, especially in the long ages when kings were sovereign. So it was with the conflict that came to a sudden conclusion at Wadi al-Makhazin, the only battle of this war. The instigator was one Dom Sebastian of the royal house of Avis, which had ruled Portugal since 1385. By the time of Sebastian's reign the Portuguese had been committing acts of aggression in Morocco and other parts of Africa for more than a century and a half. This time, however, he and his country paid dearly.

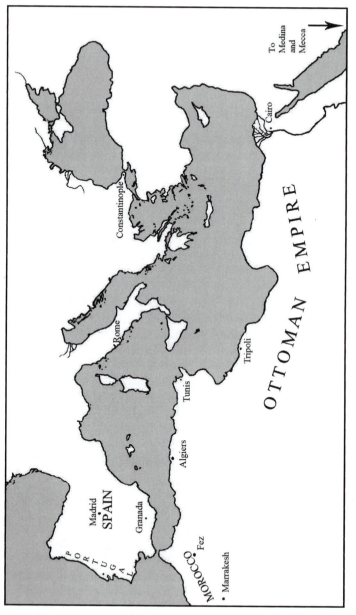

Figure 1.1 The Mediterranean Basin, Sixteenth Century, courtesy of author.

The Portuguese in Morocco

Between the medieval and the modern periods, the states that were forming on the borderlands where the Mediterranean and the Atlantic meet—Spain, Portugal, and Morocco—occupied a frontier marked by religion and culture. Christendom to the north and Islam to the south had been pushing and shoving each other across the Iberian peninsula since the eighth century in a struggle that became known on the Christian side as the Reconquista. Eventually the tide turned in favor of the Christians, and at the end of the fifteenth century the last Muslim stronghold, Granada, was swept away.

Religion became a convenient motive for justifying Portuguese imperialism in Morocco and across the African continent, but it was not the driving force. For Europe, the fifteenth century was a time of precious metal deficit, a prolonged commercial crisis known as the Great Bullion Famine. West Africa was the major supplier of gold for the Mediterranean basin, Europe, and western Asia, over trade routes stretching across the Sahara to cities in North Africa. In 1494 the Portuguese and the Spanish agreed to divide North Africa between themselves, with the Portuguese getting the Atlantic coast of Morocco and the Spanish getting the Mediterranean. The ports of Morocco became prizes in a grab for control of the major gold routes to Europe.

The Portuguese did not confine themselves to Morocco. They continued down the African coast until they reached the Costa da Mina, in the modern state of Ghana, about one hundred miles south of the Akan goldfields, the richest in West Africa. In 1482 they built a fort at Mina, from which they sent back several hundred pounds of gold annually. All the while they kept the little chunks of land they had confiscated along the Moroccan coast. In their wars against Morocco the Portuguese enjoyed certain advantages, foremost of which was an overwhelming superiority in powder weapons: cannons to sweep the fields before their forts, and muskets employed by formations of disciplined infantry.

From their outposts on the coast, the Portuguese established relations with various groups of nomadic tribesmen who hated their own central government and loved plunder more than they despised the Christian invaders. In 1515 a Portuguese force augmented by allied tribesmen struck inland, reaching the gates of Marrakesh, the country's former capital and the major city in the south. But Marrakesh held off a siege, saving the south from total occupation, and this attack proved to be the last great jolt of Portuguese aggression until Sebastian's day. After 1520, the Portuguese increasingly confined themselves to the safety of their forts, their trade dwindling and their expenses mounting. A reasonable person might have simply given in to the inevitable and ordered a general evacuation, but the Portuguese kings were usually not to be counted as such. The longer they stayed, the more they stimulated religious and patriotic backlash. In southern Morocco a family of holy men assumed the role of liberators, crushing the allies of the Portuguese and isolating the foreigners in their coastal outposts. This family, to which the three Moroccan kings who fought at Wadi al-Makhazin belonged, became the dynasty known to history as the Sa'di.

Of Marabouts and Shurafa

The Sa'dis were descended from immigrants who came from Arabia, perhaps in the twelfth century, settling in the Dar'a Valley, which lay between the Anti-Atlas Mountains and the Sahara. They were believed to have carried with them *baraka*, "blessedness," a spiritual power of divine origin. *Baraka* was inherent in acts such as a pilgrimage to Mecca. Certain words, objects, places, and people could be imbued with *baraka* as, for example, verses of the Qur'an, the holy book of Islam. Positions like *qadi*, a judge of Islamic law, and *imam*, the prayer leader in a mosque, bestowed *baraka*, or it could be earned through such virtues as learning, piety, spirituality, and philanthropy. In some places women who gave birth to twins were thought to possess *baraka*, and achieving power and wealth were assumed to be outward signs of *baraka*. It could be transmitted from one person to another, as from a teacher to a student or a preacher to a listener. Contact with infidels, however, could pollute *baraka*.

A holy man or marabout (*murabit*) was imbued with *baraka*. When the *baraka* of a particularly powerful holy man continued to linger after his death, he was recognized as a saint. Since saints were believed to enjoy a special intimacy with God, they were endowed with inherent moral qualities that made them paradigms of proper behavior. They also possessed charismatic power, and miracles involving telepathy, precognition, and clairvoyance were sometimes attributed to them. Among nomadic tribes, sainthood was passed down within certain families: *Baraka* became inherited, creating living saints. A saint with exceptional *baraka* might become the *qutb* ("pole"), the axial saint of his age, an exemplar and guide for the rest of mankind. He was thought to be the Prophet Muhammad's spiritual successor, and like the Prophet he could play the role of intercessor for Muslims on Judgment Day.

Most saints were affiliated with Sufism, a mystical esoteric knowledge dedicated to the search for personal communion with God. Sufis sought to stand "in the face of God" through extinguishing the self. Their orders were housed in fixed establishments called *zawiyas*, lodges often built around the tomb of a founding saint. The most successful *zawiyas* became centers of commercial, social, and political activity. Saints enjoyed tremendous authority over their followers, whom they could weld into highly disciplined forces. Under certain circumstances a saint could counterbalance the authority of a secular ruler or, in areas where effective government did not exist, assume that role himself.

Rivals of the marabouts in *baraka* were the *shurafa* (singular, *sharif*), the lineal descendants of Muhammad. Whereas the marabouts had to work to obtain their spiritual power, the *shurafa* derived it simply by carrying the blood of the Prophet in their veins. The Prophet's descendants were thought to be pure, even sinless, and they were believed to have direct access to their holy ancestor through their prayers. If *shurafa* could become marabouts by simply assuming the job, the reverse could also happen, and in some places the descendants of saints began to be recognized as the descendants of the Prophet Muhammad himself. If initially *sharif* and marabout were mutually exclusive classifications, by the fifteenth century the roles of marabout and *sharif* had begun to merge in the popular mind.

An individual's family origins were a serious matter in Morocco. One practical benefit was that *shurafa* were usually exempt from paying taxes. Occasionally scholars were called upon to investigate the question of who was and was not a legitimate *sharif*, but the genealogy often became so complicated a mixture of truths, half-truths, borrowed truths, and complete fabrications that no one in or out of a prominent family could untangle it sufficiently to reach a definite conclusion. On a larger scale, genealogy was the single most important factor in gauging one's social prestige and in determining who had the right to provide leadership over a community. An aspiring family could use its claim of descent from the Prophet Muhammad as the foundation on which to unite tribes, establish a dynasty, and build a state.

Morocco: From Agony to Hope

The time was ripe. At the beginning of the sixteenth century, Morocco was in an advanced state of disintegration. Large areas were under local authorities, and some places were approaching anarchy. Tribes fought each other and insecurity was widespread. The economic system was starting to break down, and Portuguese exploitation had become onerous. The central government in Fez, under the inept Wattasid dynasty, was unable to unify the country and chase out the Christian invaders. From across the land rose the cry for peace, order, and justice: Morocco begged for inspiration.

In Islamic tradition the state was expected to fulfill certain prescribed social and moral responsibilities. Individual marabouts, families of *shurafa*, and the ranks of the *zawiya* brotherhoods could transform *baraka* into physical action if the duly constituted secular power proved unjust or ineffective. Religious institutions became politicized, and the most prominent of holy men came to conclude that *baraka* qualified them for power. The call to jihad—war against unbelievers, especially those committing aggression against the Land of Islam, as the Portuguese were certainly doing—provided a power base for those who would assume command.

The fifteenth century had produced several examples of saints turned activists, the most successful of whom was Muhammad b. Sulayman al-Jazuli, founder of the Jazuliyya

Sufi order and widely recognized as the *qutb* of his time. Al-Jazuli claimed to hold conversations with God, which in effect made him a source of divine knowledge. His ideology, which came to be promoted throughout Morocco, focused on Muhammad as the ultimate model for mankind and stressed the veneration not only of the Prophet but also of his family. From this he drew the conclusion that Morocco should be ruled only by a blood descendant of the Prophet, which, not incidentally, he claimed to be—although, strictly speaking, this was unlikely given his Berber ancestry. He also believed that the ideal leader should combine spiritual and political authority. As a program of action, he preached jihad and was very successful in arousing popular support against the Portuguese, which could have been easily redirected against the ruling Wattasid Dynasty.

Al-Jazuli died suddenly in 1465, while at prayer. Some of his followers were convinced he had been poisoned by an agent of the Wattasid sultan in Fez, and they went on a rampage, raiding and plundering across southern Morocco for twenty years. As a talisman for victory, they carried with them the unburied remains of al-Jazuli in what is described as a "moveable ark." It was said to have smelled "like musk." Their rampage eventually burned out, but al-Jazuli's movement left behind a network of *zawiyas* brimming with obedient and highly motivated disciples dedicated to a creed that promoted the *shurafa* as the divinely appointed rulers of the land. This laid the ground for the rise of the Sa'dis.

The Sa'dis were but one of numerous *shurafa* families scattered around Morocco. Since their arrival in the Dar'a Valley, the Sa'dis had devoted their energies to mediating disputes among local tribes, teaching and preaching Islam, and dabbling in trans-Saharan trade. Their prominence began at the turn of the sixteenth century with the pilgrimage of the family's patriarch, Muhammad b. Abd al-Rahman al-Zaydani. On his return he spread the story that a noted holy man in Medina had predicted that his two sons were destined for great achievements and would someday rule over the people. Omens supporting the prediction were said to have followed. Not surprisingly, al-Zaydani developed a reputation as an eccentric, and in some quarters he was suspected of sorcery. Nevertheless southern

Morocco was in desperate need of leadership, and the father and his sons soon got their opportunity.

On the other side of the Anti-Atlas Mountains, in the Sus Valley, the Portuguese controlled the coast from their fort of Santa Cruz at Agadir, while inland no authority had been able to impose its will. The political situation had become so decentralized and warfare so chronic that the peasants of the region begged the local Jazulite leader to establish a stable government over them. He refused, but he told them he had heard that there was a *sharif* in the Dar'a who claimed that his sons had been prophesied to rule. They were sent for and, building on the Jazuliyya *zawiyas*, they created a movement that unified the nearby Berber tribes. In 1510, delegations from these tribes issued a formal declaration of allegiance, at which time the father assumed the appellation by which he has come to be known in history: al-Qa'im bi Amr Allah (One Who Is Risen by the Command of God), a title that was supposed to be taken by the herald of the *Mahdi*, the messianic guide who would appear as the world was coming to an end and lead the faithful to salvation. A family of saints had now taken its first step toward becoming a family of kings.

In 1511, al-Qa'im proclaimed a jihad against the Portuguese, thereby beginning a war that would drag on for decades. His immediate objective was Santa Cruz, which was promptly attacked. Portuguese artillery and muskets littered the field with dead tribesmen, teaching the Sa'dis that fanaticism and frustration were no match for gunpowder weapons. Sa'di propaganda would continue to preach jihad, but for the time being there would be no more headlong charges into the mouths of cannon. Instead the Sa'dis focused on the more difficult task of transforming their tribal confederation into a state. The Sus offered considerable potential. Nestled between the High and the Anti-Atlas Mountains, it was a rich area that produced a bounty of crops and supported numerous towns. Desperate for the return of a well-structured government, the people of the Sus agreed to provide the Sa'dis with enough revenue to create a modest-sized professional army.

Muhammad al-Qa'im died in 1518 and was buried next to al-Jazuli. He had designated his elder son, Ahmad al-A'raj (the

Lame), to be his heir and his younger son, Muhammad al-Shaykh, to be governor of the Sus. Al-Shaykh concentrated on building up the local economy, especially the cultivation and trade of sugar. In 1524, the Sa'dis became masters of the city of Marrakesh, according to one story, by conquering it outright. Another account, however, has the brothers invited there by its amir, and after an amiable chat the Sa'dis poisoned him. Whatever the case, the amir had been a vassal of the Wattasid sultan, who reacted by marching an army to Marrakesh. The Sa'dis agreed to recognize his sovereignty, and he returned to his capital at Fez to put down a revolt by his own nephews.

The Wattasids were the fourth dynasty to have ruled Morocco since it took the basic form of a country in the eleventh century. Under the first two, the Almoravids and the Almohads, the capital had been Marrakesh, but the third, the Marinids, switched the capital to Fez, where it remained under the Wattasids. Normally the Moroccan state was little more than a confederation of tribes manipulated by the sultan and his administration. Allegiance held the state together, but this was a fluctuating commodity. Out in the countryside, tribesmen lived in segmented societies loyal to a small kinship-based group rather than to a national unit. The central government could impose its will on such groups only by force, but its armies were fragile. Most of its warriors came from tribes allied with the ruling clan, who fought when it was convenient, and their chiefs could slide from sultan's ally to sultan's enemy in easy fashion. In areas where nomadic tribes were beyond its control, the central government could not collect taxes—a condition that prevailed during the fifteenth and early sixteenth centuries in most of southern Morocco.

The Moroccan state could not mobilize the Moroccan nation for war against the Portuguese because the Moroccan nation was divided within itself. When the Wattasids challenged the Portuguese, the armies of Fez usually lost, discrediting the dynasty in the eyes of its subjects and thereby perpetuating the internal weakness. Under these conditions the Sa'dis became a symbol of renewal. Building on a network of sympathizers and agents among the *shurafa* and the Sufi brotherhoods, their movement became a national one. Many saw them as the only hope for Morocco.

The Wattasids had so many problems that they did not get back to the Sa'dis until 1527, and then only after the *sharif* in Marrakesh refused to pay taxes to the sultan in Fez. War between the two continued on and off, with the Sa'dis generally getting the better of it because of an increasing supply of guns and cannons bartered from European contrabandists for Sus Valley sugar. To maintain their image as jihadist warriors, the Sa'dis also pressured the Portuguese coastal forts. In March 1541, Sa'di forces launched an all-out attack on the stronghold of Santa Cruz, during which the Portuguese munitions depot caught fire and exploded. The taking of Santa Cruz started a chain reaction: From the spoils came many new weapons, while Portuguese prisoners filled Sa'di coffers with ransom money. For the Portuguese, the loss of Santa Cruz forced the evacuation of two other major forts in the south.

The fall of Santa Cruz had a profound impact on the internal dynamics of the ruling family. The victory belonged to the younger brother, Muhammad al-Shaykh, but when al-A'raj demanded a cut, as was his right as head of state, a short civil war ensued. It was decided in two battles in which the numerically superior tribal cavalry from Marrakesh was mowed down by the musket and cannon fire of the men from the Sus. Muhammad al-Shaykh emerged victorious, and al-A'raj went into internal exile in the oasis of Tafilalt on the border of the Sahara.

Morocco Reunified: The Reign of Muhammad al-Shaykh

Muhammad al-Shaykh was an exceptional individual, described by one chronicler of his dynasty as "a man of swift decision, firm resolution and lofty purpose; of imposing aspect, and great vigour and energy. . . . He was one of the favoured of fortune, devoted to the holy war, possessor of a white hand in Islam." He loved poetry, knew the Qur'an by heart, and could debate Islamic law with the jurisconsults. He was also ruthlessly ambitious. He claimed leadership over the worldwide jihad on the basis of his sharifian blood, yet in a world crazed by religious passion, he was no fanatic. To his enemies, the Portuguese, he was a man of honor; to his co-religionists, the Ottoman Turks, he was a canker.

that is a great word.

Muhammad al-Shaykh had no intention of remaining the ruler of half a country. The capture of Santa Cruz proved to be a great blow against the Wattasids in the battle for Moroccan public opinion, and with his older brother safely out of the way, he resumed the war with Fez in 1544. By this time the Wattasids were no match, and to save his dynasty, the Wattasid ruler, Abu Hasun, sent a message of submission to the far-off sultan of the Ottoman Empire, Sulayman the Magnificent, who was never one to pass up an opportunity to acquire a new country. Sulayman thought the idea of adding Morocco to his domains an excellent one, and he dispatched an envoy to Marrakesh to demand that al-Shaykh back off from the war and join the Wattasids in officially recognizing the Ottoman sultan as overlord.

Muhammad al-Shaykh did not take bullying well, and he had developed a strong distaste for Turks. The sources are unclear as to whether the Turkish envoy was executed; if not, he came very close to it. And to press the point, Muhammad al-Shaykh resumed his offensive in the north, taking Fez at the beginning of 1549. The reunification of Morocco, however, did not ensure its survival. The geopolitical world of the sixteenth century was precarious for little polities like Morocco, caught between the proverbial rock and a hard place in the form of Spain on the one side and the Ottoman Empire on the other.

Next door to Morocco, the Turks had been in control in Algiers since 1518, when local corsairs, the so-called Barbary pirates, offered territory they had seized to Sultan Selim the Grim, Sulayman the Magnificent's predecessor. But if Selim the Grim and Sulayman the Magnificent thought they had gotten something for nothing, they were wrong. North Africa was less an opportunity than a trap that brought the Turks head-to-head with another imperial power that had been building its own empire from the other direction. The Spanish had been expanding eastward along the Mediterranean coast in much the same way the Portuguese were doing on the Atlantic, the Spanish forts ultimately reaching as far as Tripoli. In 1535, Tunis, the greatest city on the North African coast west of Egypt, was taken by Spain. The Mediterranean could have become as Spanish as the Caribbean were it not for the arrival of the Turks. For much of the rest of the century, the two superpowers fought a debilitating duel that neither would win. In the meantime, the prognosis for an independent Morocco did not look good except that both superpowers considered it a convenient buffer against the other.

Initially, the Ottomans had shown little inclination to absorb Morocco. To conquer and rule it directly may have been more than the thinly stretched Turks were prepared to do. And since the Turkish presence in North Africa was not the result of some master plan for conquest, the next step after Algiers was not necessarily Fez or Marrakesh. Thus the Ottomans did not take immediate action when Muhammad al-Shaykh unified the country. Nevertheless, the Wattasid offer had piqued their interest. In January 1552, Sulayman the Magnificent sent a letter to Muhammad al-Shaykh appealing for Islamic solidarity. He offered Turkish friendship and support, but Muhammad al-Shaykh would have had to recognize the Ottoman sultan as his overlord, which could have meant little more than printing the Turkish ruler's name on coins, saying the Friday prayer in his name, and perhaps paying a nominal tribute or sending extravagant gifts on occasion. The *sharif*, however, did not so much as respond.

Eventually, policymakers in the Ottoman capital of Constantinople began thinking about Morocco in more aggressive terms. If the Turks could extend their control across the whole North African coast, they would gain a foothold on the Atlantic, thereby opening a new world of opportunity. In this case, the Turks had no interest in seeing a strong Morocco, which meant keeping the decadent Wattasid dynasty in power and the more vigorous Sa'di one out. When Abu Hasun, who had escaped the fall of his capital, requested assistance, it was provided. Early in 1554, a Turkish army marched on Fez and dislodged Muhammad al-Shaykh. But the Turks were not yet prepared to stay in Morocco indefinitely, and when their army departed, Muhammad al-Shaykh retook the city and killed Abu Hasun. As for Sulayman the Magnificent, he had more pressing matters in southeastern Europe and southwestern Asia. For the time being, Morocco wasn't worth the effort of a major campaign.

If the reunification of Morocco under its new dynasty settled old issues, changing conditions soon produced new ones. The rugged, warlike Berbers of the mountains and the desert had been quick to support the Sa'dis when they represented anti-establishment forces. That situation changed in 1554. After the Sa'dis assumed control over the central authority, tribesmen reacted to them in the way they had traditionally treated sovereigns: by ignoring them or, when pushed, by revolting. Other matters changed as well. The Sa'dis had risen by exploiting the wave of religion-inspired anger unleashed by Portuguese and Spanish aggression even if the Sa'dis had, in fact, directed much of their military effort against fellow Moroccans. However, once he had taken control, Muhammad al-Shaykh no longer saw the Portuguese and Spanish as his principal threat. While it remained official policy to despise the Christians and preach jihad against them, the *sharif* considered the Turks a more dangerous enemy and began to negotiate in secret with the Spanish.

Muhammad al-Shaykh's fear of the Turks was more than an unwarranted case of paranoia; the Ottoman Empire was not simply a bigger version of Morocco. The Ottomans had built a variant of the modern state, complete with a settled tax base, a bureaucracy, a navy, and a gunpowder-equipped professional army. Such a state was a threat not just to the Sa'di dynasty but to the existence of Morocco itself. A Morocco conquered by Spain or Portugal would have constituted an indigestible lump that would have had to come out sooner or later; Morocco was not Granada. But the Turks were Muslims, and Muslims in other parts of their empire had discovered that Ottoman rule was reasonable, even enlightened, compared with that of most native rulers. Morocco could have been absorbed into the Ottoman Empire.

For the Sa'dis, the issue was as much ideological as political. They claimed to be the lineal descendants of the Prophet, while the Ottomans weren't even Arabs. To project a messianic image as the leader of the Muslims, Muhammad al-Shaykh bestowed on himself the exalted title of Mahdi, though he did not press the issue with theological arguments to support his claim. Al-Shaykh is reported to have said he would not rest until the Turks had been driven out of Egypt—an idle boast, but one that infuriated Sulayman the Magnificent. When an Ottoman ambassador brought letters from Sulayman addressed to the "Shaykh of the Arab Tribes," putting al-Shaykh on a level with tribal chiefs, the Sa'di *sharif* returned the insult by referring to the Ottoman sultan as the "King of the Fishermen."

The Spanish were delighted. With Protestants and perfidious French to the north and Turks to the east, the Spanish in the sixteenth century feared encirclement by their enemies. Many in Madrid and Rome suspected that the eventual goal of these enemies was not just to dismember Spain but to eradicate Roman Catholicism. Following the Sa'di unification of Morocco in 1548–1549, alarmists in Madrid were predicting an invasion of their own country. Instead, Muhammad al-Shaykh ordered an excursion into nearby Ottoman territory, an unsuccessful attempt to capture the city of Tlemcen. A period of détente between Morocco and Spain followed, at times appearing to be almost an informal alliance. But Morocco and Spain could not become fast friends. Religion, geography, and history determined that they should be antagonists; only politics brought them together, in a relationship that at times must have seemed maddeningly entangled. In the ongoing war between Morocco and Portugal, the Spanish could always be counted on to favor their cousins while the Moroccans were suspected of aiding the underground community of Spanish Muslims in Granada. For Morocco, if the Spanish were not quite the threat that the Turks were in the mid-sixteenth century, events could quickly change that. If Spain was to be used to counter the Ottomans, something was needed to balance Spain.

Fortunately for Morocco, unity was no more evident among Christians than among Muslims. Spain's ambitions were checked by its enemies in Europe, especially France and England. Because France was an old friend of the Ottomans, Morocco preferred England, and the two states enjoyed a period of friendship and trade that stretched to the end of the century. Ideologically, each side had to convince itself that Roman Catholicism as represented by Spain was worse than the religion of its newfound friend. Nevertheless, neither government could appear to be too friendly toward the other; public opinion on such a volatile issue could cause more problems than the connection was worth.

Al-Shaykh's English tie never annoyed the Spanish enough to make them drop their alignment with Morocco against the Ottoman Empire. His Spanish connection, however, grated on the Turks. When Muhammad al-Shaykh flippantly remarked to Sulayman the Magnificent's ambassador, "Tell your master that I am coming to invade his country," the Ottomans decided the Shaykh had gone too far. A number of Turkish soldiers showed up at the Sa'di court, claiming to be deserters. They proved to be excellent troops, and their ruse was so convincing that Muhammad al-Shaykh made them his bodyguard. However, they had orders from the Turkish pasha in Algiers to eliminate him. Their opportunity came in October 1557, while the *sharif* was leading an expedition against tribesmen in the High Atlas Mountains. One night Muhammad al-Shaykh's Turkish bodyguards killed him in front of his tent and cut off his head. They were in turn hunted down and killed, all but one or two who reached Algiers carrying the head in a bag of bran and salt, which was sent on to Constantinople.

By pointing his country in directions that his more famous son, Ahmad al-Mansur, would later go, Muhammad al-Shaykh was a pivotal figure in the history of Morocco. His political and diplomatic policies, however, too often appeared at odds with his dynasty's professed ideological goals, leaving contradictions that would never be reconciled. After coming to power under the banner of revolution and religious fervor, the Sa'dis found they had to conform to very different geopolitical practicalities. For the foreseeable future, jihad would be relegated more to the realm of talk than action.

A CLOSER LOOK

Moroccan sources used to study the Sa'di dynasty

The work of the Moroccan historian Muhammad al-Saghir b. al-Hajj Muhammad b. Abd Allah al-Ifrani is considered the most important source for the history of the Sa'di dynasty. Al-Ifrani's book, *Nuzhat al Hadj* (translated as *Histoire de la Dynastie Saadienne au Maroc*), was written in the early eighteenth century. Its author occupied a position in the royal court of the dynasty that followed the Sa'dis, which gave him access to much primary source material, including letters and government documents that are no longer available. Al-Ifrani also used earlier works written by chroniclers who lived under the Sa'dis, chief of whom was Abd al-Aziz al-Fishtali, Sultan Ahmad al-Mansur's secretary in charge of royal correspondence and his official court poet. Al-Fishtali's history, *Manahil al-Safa* (*Founts of Purity*), is reported to have originally comprised eight volumes, part of which has survived in its original form. Also, large chunks of al-Fishtali's work lie buried in the work of others, particularly al-Ifrani.

Al-Fishtali is the most primary of sources because he was an eyewitness and often a participant in the events he recorded. He had access to privileged information that has long since disappeared. Yet the great disadvantage in using al-Fishtali is that he was a panegyrist, a writer whose job was to praise the ruler in poetry and prose. Court panegyrists were rewarded in accordance with the level of their flattery rather than the degree of their accuracy. *Manahil al-Safa* was intended to be the definitive work on the Sa'di dynasty, the official view that Sultan Ahmad al-Mansur wanted posterity to take of himself and those who came before him. No clear lines were drawn between history and biography on the one side and hagiography, genealogy, literature, and propaganda on the other. It was, as one later historian quipped, "history paid for by the king." When it came to basic factual material, however, outright lies were frowned upon. Court chroniclers generally did not make up history; rather, they interpreted it from a decided viewpoint.

Al-Ifrani also used the *Tarikh al-dawla al-Sa'diyya* (translated as *Sur la dynastie Sa'dienne du Maroc*), by an anonymous author thought to be from the city of Fez. This was likely written in the mid to late seventeenth century, after the Sa'di dynasty had come to its dreadful end, and the work may serve as something of a dark obituary on it. This work is the earliest example of nonofficial history written on the Sa'dis, and it might be labeled "the other side of Moroccan history." It is a sad, relentless tale of lies, intrigues, plots, persecutions, murders, and unnecessary or aggressive wars, all in all a bitter denunciation of the Sa'dis for their blunders, brutalities, and abuses. Al-Ifrani called this work a "virulent diatribe" but used it to counteract works like that of al-Fishtali. Some of its information is impossible to verify because the so-called Anonymous Chronicler of Fez is the only source to report it, but he often does so in such detail as to be convincing. The reader must be cautious: The Anonymous

Chronicler of Fez has a tendency to report rumor as fact and is particularly attracted to conspiracy theories. His specialty was digging up depreciative tidbits on the Sa'dis, but the Turks and the Christians were fair game as well. If in the Anonymous Chronicler gossip becomes history, doubtless some gossip from this period probably was more accurate than al-Fishtali's official version of history. And it remains a useful work today, for the *Tarikh al-dawla al-Sa'diyya* has survived relatively intact.

Al-Ifrani is sometimes accused of being an apologist for the Sa'di dynasty, a charge that is probably unfair. No doubt he had a generally positive attitude toward his subject, and he does pause, for example, to scold the Anonymous Chronicler of Fez when he thinks that author has crossed the line between legitimate criticism and character assassination. But al-Ifrani had no reason to flatter the Sa'dis, who were long gone by his time, and the dynasty he worked under held a negative view of them. Writing a century after al-Fishtali and a half century after the Anonymous Chronicler of Fez, al-Ifrani had a clearer perspective and could take a more balanced view of what had gone on. Given the conditions under which history was written in his time, al-Ifrani casts an amazingly critical eye.

The most recent source of note is Abu al-Qasim al-Zayyani, who wrote in the last decade of the eighteenth century. Like al-Ifrani, he worked as an official for the dynasty that succeeded the Sa'dis, only at a higher level. He was the first Moroccan historian to attempt a universal history stretching from Adam to the Ottomans. In this the Sa'dis are given a chapter, of which al-Mansur occupies somewhat less than half. Al-Zayyani was more interested in al-Mansur's Songhay venture than in the larger geopolitical issues involving the Ottoman Empire, Spain, and England. He took much from al-Fishtali and al-Ifrani but includes some very precise details that must have come from archival material now lost. Despite several glaring errors, especially on figures or dating, his work has valuable information on matters al-Fishtali, al-Ifrani, and the Anonymous Chronicler of Fez ignored. This may have been intentional; al-Zayyani may have been trying to fill the gaps in earlier accounts.

Abu l'Abbas Ahmad:
The Early Years

Abu l'Abbas Ahmad was born in Fez in 1549, the youngest of eight sons of Muhammad al-Shaykh. The Timbuktu chronicler Abd al-Rahman al-Sadi claims that Ahmad's mother was a Fulbe concubine, that is, a Sudanese slave from Muhammad al-Shaykh's harem. Children inherited solely from their father—their mother's status, in theory, did not matter—and many a Moroccan sultan came from slave women, Sudanese or otherwise. A Spanish priest, Father Luis Nieto, who knew Ahmad, described him as "black in color." Al-Ifrani gives Ahmad's mother's name as Lalla (an honorific title, roughly "My Lady") Mas'uda, and Ibn al-Qadi, a writer employed by the sharifian court, refers to her as Awda b. Abd Allah al-Wazgiti al-Warzazati. He and al-Fishtali claim that she was of high birth, and a plaque on her tomb describes her as a woman of noble origins.

Al-Fishtali also maintains that prophecies foretold Ahmad's greatness. According to one of them, a revered holy man in far-away Cairo predicted to a Moroccan pilgrim that Muhammad al-Shaykh's youngest son, Ahmad, would become Caliph of Islam (worldwide leader of all Muslims) even though the pilgrim was not aware that Ahmad had even been born. Upon his return home, the pilgrim conveyed this prediction to Muhammad al-Shaykh, who did not act surprised in the least.

During Ahmad's early years, a number of people were said to have proclaimed him the most promising of Muhammad

The Sa'di Dynasty

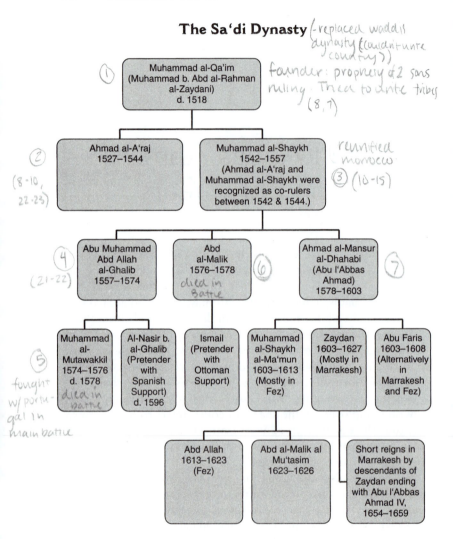

(handwritten annotations):
- replaced waddis dynasty (couldn't unite country?)
- founder: prophecy of 2 sons ruling. Tried to unite tribes (8, 7)
- ① Muhammad al-Qa'im
- ② (8-10, 22-23) Ahmad al-A'raj 1527–1544
- ③ (10-15) reunified morocco — Muhammad al-Shaykh
- ④ (21-22) Abu Muhammad Abd Allah al-Ghalib
- ⑥ died in battle — Abd al-Malik
- ⑦ Ahmad al-Mansur al-Dhahabi
- ⑤ fought w/ portugal in main battle — Muhammad al-Mutawakkil, died in battle

Tree contents:

- ① Muhammad al-Qa'im (Muhammad b. Abd al-Rahman al-Zaydani) d. 1518
  - ② Ahmad al-A'raj 1527–1544
  - ③ Muhammad al-Shaykh 1542–1557 (Ahmad al-A'raj and Muhammad al-Shaykh were recognized as co-rulers between 1542 & 1544.)
    - ④ Abu Muhammad Abd Allah al-Ghalib 1557–1574
      - ⑤ Muhammad al-Mutawakkil 1574–1576 d. 1578
      - Al-Nasir b. al-Ghalib (Pretender with Spanish Support) d. 1596
    - ⑥ Abd al-Malik 1576–1578
      - Ismail (Pretender with Ottoman Support)
    - ⑦ Ahmad al-Mansur al-Dhahabi (Abu l'Abbas Ahmad) 1578–1603
      - Muhammad al-Shaykh al-Ma'mun 1603–1613 (Mostly in Fez)
        - Abd Allah 1613–1623 (Fez)
        - Abd al-Malik al Mu'tasim 1623–1626
      - Zaydan 1603–1627 (Mostly in Marrakesh)
        - Short reigns in Marrakesh by descendants of Zaydan ending with Abu l'Abbas Ahmad IV, 1654–1659
      - Abu Faris 1603–1608 (Alternatively in Marrakesh and Fez)

Figure 2.1 The Sa'di Dynasty, courtesy of author.

al-Shaykh's progeny, including his father, who, according to al-Ifrani, "recognized him as the most remarkable of his children." In one instance, Ahmad reportedly invaded his father's council chamber during a meeting and made such an impression that the sultan asked one of his councilors to carry the boy off on his shoulders in triumph. Al-Fishtali believes Ahmad himself knew at an early age that he would become a great leader, and he began to prepare himself for that role.

The Reign of Abd Allah al-Ghalib

Whatever Muhammad al-Shaykh might have thought about his youngest son, he had no intention of bypassing his older sons in the succession. Before Ahmad could assume the throne, he had to wait out the reigns of three other members of his family. First, however, Morocco itself had to be secured. The Turks took advantage of the unsettled conditions created by the death of al-Shaykh, but their invasion was stopped at the Battle of Wadi Laban. They then retreated, fearing the Spanish would cut their lines. The sharifian dynasty had been saved, courtesy of the infidels.

The Turks did not return after Wadi Laban, leaving the House of Sa'di firmly on the throne and Morocco unified under Muhammad al-Shaykh's oldest son, Abu Muhammad Abd Allah al-Ghalib. His most lasting legacy was his great building projects, especially the restoration and beautification of Marrakesh, done in an ostentatious style heavily influenced by Andalusian architecture, with a great new mosque, the Mawwasin or "Mosque of the Sharifs," as centerpiece. In his domestic policy, al-Ghalib guided to completion the transition that had begun under his father. The Sa'dis had risen to power as the revolutionary leaders of a mass movement; now they were the establishment. The masses would have to be demobilized and controlled through propaganda. In return, al-Ghalib's reign brought stability and prosperity.

Moroccan foreign policy under al-Ghalib has been subject to varying interpretations. According to one, he made no effort to improve relations with the Turks although he did not intentionally antagonize them. Another sees him as having learned the lesson of his father's assassination, which led him to defuse the volatile situation with the Turks and even quietly to recognize

Ottoman supremacy. For Morocco, the specter of war faded for the time being. On the wider international scene, the last decade of al-Ghalib's reign witnessed two enormous events that would affect all the states bordering the Mediterranean: the Battle of Lepanto in 1571 and the capture and recapture of Tunis between 1569 and 1574.

Lepanto, fought off the coast of Greece and involving more than four hundred galleys, was a spectacular victory for Spain and its allies over the Ottoman fleet. Among its many consequences was the cancellation of plans some elements within the Ottoman government were developing for an invasion of Morocco. Tunis was captured by the Turks in 1569, retaken by the Spanish in 1573, and recaptured the following year by an Ottoman land-and-sea force. This signaled the beginning of the end of the Spanish coastal fort system in North Africa. Lepanto and Tunis had evened the score and led to a stalemate. Neither side would be able to win the war; the only question was how long it would take for both of them to figure this out.

Abd Allah means "Servant of God," a name al-Ghalib took very seriously. He was by all accounts an extraordinarily pious individual. Even the contemporary Turkish historian Mustafa al-Jannabi, no friend of the House of Sa'di, called him "knowledgeable" and "intimate with the scholars." Many in the Moroccan religious establishment recognized him as a saint, and some considered him the *qutb*. Unlike his father, however, he did not presume to take the title of Mahdi. He was said to have died of natural causes brought on by excessive fasting in the year the Turks took Tunis for the final time.

A Question of Succession

Along with his great piety, al-Ghalib has been described as being modest and gentle. Nevertheless, he began his reign with the horrible massacre of his uncle, Ahmad al-A'raj, and al-A'raj's entire family down to the smallest child (al-Zayyani claims that the order for this actually was sent out by Muhammad al-Shaykh just before his death). Al-Ghalib's surviving brothers, Abd al-Mu'min, Abd al-Malik, and Ahmad may have lived in Tafilalt for a while, but at an uncertain time they crossed over into

Ottoman territory. Under the conventions by which states dealt with each other, it was common for one to exploit the intrafamily problems of another by harboring pretenders, usually younger brothers, disgruntled sons, or nephews of the current monarch. If an excuse became necessary for invading one's neighbor, support of a pretender was often used. The Ottomans and even the Spanish kept a larder full of Sa'di, and before them Wattasid, pretenders for potential use.

The Sa'di system of succession, which had originated with Muhammad al-Qa'im, would remain a problem until the end of the dynasty. In theory, the right to rule was to go from oldest male to next oldest male, which meant that the leadership would pass through a line of brothers before it went to the next generation. In overthrowing Ahmad al-A'raj and recognizing his own son as heir, Muhammad al-Shaykh had transgressed this system, although he appears to have favored it when regarding his own sons and their heirs. Al-Ghalib chose to follow the example rather than the theory.

In Algiers, al-Ghalib's brothers were welcomed. Abd al-Mu'min was appointed governor of Tlemcen, the major city in Ottoman territory closest to Morocco. When al-Ghalib looked across the border, the Turks wanted him to see his potential replacement. In 1572, Abd al-Mu'min was assassinated by a Moroccan agent while at prayer in a mosque, probably on orders from al-Ghalib's son, Muhammad al-Mutawakkil.

The second oldest brother, Abu Marwan Abd al-Malik ("the Servant of the King"), served the Ottoman sultan mostly as a holy warrior. He was captured at Lepanto and spent a year in Spanish captivity, during which he learned to speak Spanish and gained an appreciation of some aspects of European culture. Afterward he returned to Algiers and made a trip to Constantinople with his mother and brother Ahmad in an unsuccessful attempt to solicit help in capturing the Moroccan throne. During the taking of Tunis, Abd al-Malik commanded a ship and was conspicuous for his bravery. The brothers were the first to bring news of the victory to Constantinople, for which they were rewarded, according to al-Zayyani, with an order directing the authorities in Algiers to provide them with the military assistance they had earlier requested.

Al-Fishtali, however, tells a different story. According to him, at the time Muhammad al-Shaykh proclaimed al-Ghalib as his heir, he extracted a promise from al-Ghalib to watch over and protect Ahmad. Muhammad al-Shaykh is reputed to have called Ahmad "the centerpiece of the necklace of his children." Subsequently al-Ghalib honored his father's wishes, and Ahmad remained safe in Morocco until the end of al-Ghalib's reign.

Two Short Reigns

Before his death, al-Ghalib saw to it that the throne bypassed his surviving brothers and went to his son, Abu Abd Allah Muhammad al-Mutawakkil ("One Who Relies on God"). If Ahmad had indeed spent the al-Ghalib years in Morocco, he now had the good sense to get out quickly. As al-Fishtali tells it, Ahmad fled with a small army across the desert separating Morocco and Algeria, during which his soldiers suffered from a lack of food and water. Some of the fainthearted grumbled mutiny, but Ahmad calmly went hunting, killed some game, and roasted it. When they saw his composure, the men regained their confidence and renewed their loyalty to him.

The Turkish garrison in Algiers, as it turned out, was happy to oblige the two brothers, providing they promised a large payment in gold on the completion of the task. The Turks may not have had a good feeling about Muhammad al-Mutawakkil, who was a man of contradictions. He has been depicted as a gentle soul, a reader of books, and a poet of some ability, but he was also a persecutor of Christians who had the misfortune of falling into his hands, and he was known to mistreat Jews as well. Al-Jannabi says of him that in his "pursuit in the command of holy war against the Europeans [he] was not exceeded by anyone." Nevertheless, he was not considered a friend of the Turks. He had once insulted the Ottoman ambassador, and the Turks may have suspected that he was behind the Abd al-Mu'min assassination. It was not inconceivable that the young sultan might turn to the Spanish despite his personal dislike of Christians. If the Ottomans did establish Abd al-Malik in Marrakesh, and he proved a suitable client, Morocco could be used as a base to extend the war closer to Spain and perhaps out into the Atlantic.

Abd al-Malik's invasion force engaged the Moroccan army under Muhammad al-Mutawakkil south of Fez. While al-Mutawakkil had been reading books and writing poems, Abd al-Malik had been spending his time secretly negotiating with Sa'id al-Dughali, the commander of al-Mutawakkil's best infantry unit, the Andalusian musketeers. As a result, when the two armies met, the Andalusians quickly changed sides, and the battle ended almost before it began. When al-Mutawakkil realized what had happened, he quickly exited the field, and enough of his army followed to regroup for a second go-round.

Abd al-Malik entered Fez on March 31, 1576. Having settled in, he paid off the Turks and sent them back to Algiers. His own army, consisting of the Andalusians who had defected plus Berber and Arab tribesmen, marched south to finish off al-Mutawakkil, although the sources appear at variance as to whether Abd al-Malik or Ahmad was now leading them. The deciding battle took place in July, and again it was brief. The brothers' army opened with a tremendous artillery barrage that blew al-Mutawakkil's men off the field. Al-Mutawakkil took flight, stopping briefly in Marrakesh, then retreating into the mountains. Ahmad was assigned the task of pursuing and destroying him, and for about a year the two armies chased each other around the southern part of the country, mostly in and out of the Sus Valley. The details of this campaign come chiefly from al-Fishtali, who makes the most of Ahmad's first opportunity at a major command.

Al-Fishtali emphasizes Ahmad's tactical brilliance, his leadership, and above all his bravery. In one instance Ahmad cleverly induces some Turkish mercenaries to change sides, even if the mercenaries left in al-Mutawakkil's employ were doubtless anxious by this time to cut their best deal with the side that had obviously won the war. Ahmad is credited with defeating al-Mutawakkil despite his nephew's superior force. However, it is clear that al-Mutawakkil's army had quickly been whittled down to little more than a band of brigands numbering less than a thousand, which is probably why they were successful in slipping through Ahmad's hands again and again. The accolades of al-Fishtali notwithstanding, Ahmad was not successful in completing his mission. After doing some damage to the

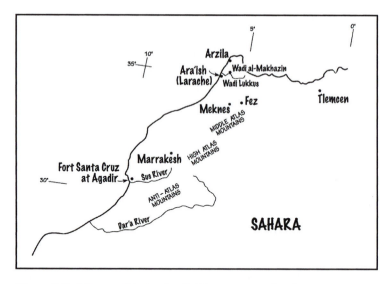

Figure 2.2   Morocco Under the Sa'dis, courtesy of author.

sugar industry in the Sus, al-Mutawakkil moved north in search of European assistance.

Morocco was now firmly in the Ottoman camp, or so it seemed. But Abd al-Malik was not a man to be underestimated. He proved to be a politician of extraordinary cunning: Urbane, debonair, charming, and disarming, he played a double-dealing game. He convinced the Ottomans of his intentions to serve as a loyal client. Friday prayers were said in the Ottoman sultan's name, and the Moroccan army and government were reorganized using Turkish models. Abd al-Malik dressed in Turkish clothes, spoke Turkish in court, and sent gifts and flattering letters to the sultan in Constantinople. But Morocco hardly became an appendage of the Ottoman Empire, and Turkish military and administrative officials were not permanently stationed there. Behind the scenes, Abd al-Malik opened the old tie with Spain, going so far as to offer a secret treaty with a clear anti-Ottoman slant. His policy paid a quick dividend. When al-Mutawakkil showed up in Spanish territory begging assistance, the Spanish king, Philip II, ordered him expelled. For al-Mutawakkil, only Sebastian, King of Portugal, was left.

Sebastian and the Last Crusade

An energetic royal family had played no small role in the rise of Portugal's empire in the fifteenth century, just as in the sixteenth century a series of incapable or indifferent kings led the country's fortunes downhill. When Sebastian assumed power in 1568 at the age of fifteen, he was the last of his line. His most immediate task should have been to marry a suitable princess and begin producing heirs. But the young king had grown up under the tutelage of reactionary advisers who filled his head with romantic notions and the lust for righteous battle. He didn't have time for women, whom he did not seem to like in any case. God, he believed, had ordained more important matters for him. As a man, Sebastian was brave and forthright, a prince of impeccable honor and chivalrous intentions. But he was also inflexible and had a bad case of tunnel vision. For him, war against evil was preferable to peace, and a crusade against unbelievers was the best of all wars. He did not seem to care that the situation involving Portugal and Morocco and their larger neighbors, Spain and the Ottoman Empire, had become complex. To him, a Moor was a Moor. Given the world of sixteenth-century international politics, Sebastian's ideas were simplistic to a dangerous degree.

At age twenty-one, Sebastian sneaked away from the court, boarded a ship, and sailed to the Portuguese fort at Ceuta in northern Morocco. From there and nearby Tangier, he and a small party of equally imprudent noblemen sought adventure by riding around the countryside and challenging any Moroccans they came across. The astounded Moroccans finally amassed a sizeable force, which Sebastian and his men attacked even though they were greatly outnumbered. Most of Sebastian's companions were slain; the king, fighting impossible odds, somehow made it back to safety.

Not long thereafter, al-Mutawakkil appeared in Portuguese territory appealing for help. In February 1578 he met with Sebastian in Lisbon and struck a deal. Sebastian's price was the entire Moroccan coastline, with al-Mutawakkil keeping the interior as a protectorate. That almost everyone at the Portuguese court whose opinion was worthy of consideration advised Sebastian against an invasion did not dishearten him. He was king; if he was determined to do something, he would do it, however irresponsible. Sebastian lived just prior to the advent of the great absolutist monarchs of Europe, and he displayed pronounced tendencies in that direction. Absolute monarchs could make absolutely idiotic decisions and engage in absolutely asinine behavior, and there was little anyone could do about it. Before leaving Portugal, Sebastian had a crown and royal regalia made for his coronation as King of Morocco.

Outside the court, Sebastian's most important relative, his uncle, Philip II of Spain, had strong misgivings. Philip II and Sebastian may have shared some ancestors, but they were not formed from the same mold. Philip was solitary and secretive, a plodder rather than a visionary, a cautious and calculating monarch. He must have suspected that his nephew was not entirely of sound mind. But Sebastian was of his blood and his faith. In response to Sebastian's nagging, Philip finally agreed to provide five thousand infantry. Shortly thereafter Philip entered negotiations with Abd al-Malik that led to a détente between their two countries.

Far more important than the covert friendship between Madrid and Marrakesh was Spain's relationship with the Ottoman Empire. In 1575 the Spanish state had gone bankrupt despite the treasure of the Americas. Philip must have concluded that it was time to cut his losses, beginning with the war against the Turks. The Spanish opened secret negotiations with the Ottomans that could have been jeopardized by a Portuguese attack on Morocco aided by Spain. Philip now stepped up his attempt to dissuade Sebastian, but to no avail even after Philip threatened to withdraw his troops. Sebastian did get one strong vote in his favor: Pope Gregory XIII gave the expedition his blessing, officially dubbing it a "crusade."

The Gathering of Armies

The Portuguese military establishment was scattered around Asia, Africa, and the New World, so Sebastian would have to create his own army from scratch. Ten to twelve thousand men were mustered, some from the ranks of unemployed laborers, but most of the soldiers were conscripts too poor to bribe their way out.

Nobles were pressured to join with the threat of having their incomes confiscated. A sizeable number of gentlemen did volunteer, seeing an opportunity to be noticed by the king; they were organized as a unit of three thousand infantry labeled the Adventurers.

The foreigners came from three directions. A brigade of two to three thousand mercenaries that had been operating in the Netherlands was hired. They were fierce and battle-hardened but unruly and predacious; the Portuguese referred to them as "the Germans." A rebel Englishman named Thomas Stukeley commanded a smaller and less troublesome unit of six hundred Italian mercenaries on loan from Pope Gregory. The final touch was provided by Philip. Sebastian had learned about his uncle's negotiations with the Turks and had demanded to be included. Philip declined, but to keep his intemperate nephew from complaining too loudly, he restored between two and three thousand troops.

Once landed, the Portuguese would be joined by al-Mutawakkil's followers. Sebastian's force was a strange aggregation, parts of it very good, other parts very bad. It was woefully overweighted in favor of infantry: The Portuguese would land with less than two thousand cavalry. Contemporary Moroccan sources, as well as al-Zayyani, put the invading force at 100,000 or more, but modern estimates range between twenty and twenty-six thousand, with thirty-six artillery pieces.

The expedition got under way in June 1578, the worst time of the year to campaign in Morocco because of the scorching heat. The initial objective was the Atlantic port of Larache (Ara'ish), but the fleet landed at Arzila, about twenty miles north. There a letter from Abd al-Malik caught up with Sebastian, a final attempt to dissuade the young crusader. Abd al-Malik called the invasion "an injustice and an act of aggression without reason, for I wish you no ill, think no evil of you and have taken no evil action against you." He offered to negotiate an agreement person to person: "I do all this in order to save you from destruction."

Reasoning with fanatics, as Abd al-Malik probably knew—Morocco had its share of them—was fruitless. But fanatics could be manipulated, so when Sebastian landed, Abd al-Malik sent a second letter: "You have already shown proof of [your] courage in leaving your country and crossing the sea to come to this country. If now you will stay in place until I can come to meet you, it is because you are a true and brave Christian; if not you are only a dog, the son of a dog." Sebastian appeared not to have had a real plan, and Abd al-Malik seemed to be issuing a challenge on the field of honor. Al-Mutawakkil, joined by the more experienced voices in the Portuguese war council, warned that it was a trick. Sebastian, however, was accustomed to ignoring good advice, so the Portuguese army stayed put for nineteen days, giving Abd al-Malik plenty of time to assemble a great army.

If anything could pull together the disparate forces of Morocco, it was a Christian invasion, and Abd al-Malik took full advantage of the situation by calling for a jihad. The "Northerners" who rendezvoused at Fez and the "Southerners" who rendezvoused at Marrakesh were contingents drawn from tribesmen whose chiefs owed allegiance to the sultan. The Moroccan army had a strong equestrian orientation, and in the approaching battle it would enjoy a decided advantage in cavalry. The prestige units were composed of light cavalrymen armed with swords, daggers, short lances, and throwing javelins. From the larger cities like Fez and Meknes came militias, mostly archers and gunmen. The men of the Sus, including a unit of musketeers, continued to be the backbone of the Sa'di army, at least as far as native troops went. Together, these forces constituted the traditional sector of the Moroccan army.

Tribal contingents would be necessary in a large-scale melee, but Sebastian's army had some very fine troops capable of scattering a much larger, disorganized mass. For the Moroccans to win, they would have to depend on a modernized core of professionals to stand toe-to-toe against the Europeans. Then the weight of the tribal cavalry could be used to wear down the smaller force. By 1578 this core was in place, and it was very good, a match for European forces of equal size. The weapon of choice for the professional part of Abd al-Malik's army was the arquebus, a heavy shoulder gun with a slow-burning matchlock fixed on its gunstock. Against the Portuguese the sultan could send about three thousand arquebusiers with an additional thousand mounted gunmen known as spahis. The professional army was built around Turks, Andalusians, and renegades.

Turkish soldiers in North Africa resembled the storied Janissary Corps, except that they had been recruited as adult volunteers in the Turkish heartland. They were accomplished in the use of firearms, highly disciplined, and usually very effective. Turkish mercenaries began to appear in Moroccan armies in the late 1530s, usually as small companies of arquebusiers. Occasionally, when Ottoman and Sa'dian interests intersected, Turkish regulars from Algiers fought alongside the Moroccans.

Abd al-Malik had no intention of becoming too dependent on Turks, regular or hired, so he used Andalusians and renegades as a counterbalance. The renegades (known in Morocco as *uluj*) were European Christians who had converted to Islam. Virtually every nationality from Scottish to Hungarian was represented, but in Morocco the largest group was Spanish, and in some units of the Moroccan army, Spanish was the language of discourse. Renegades came from a variety of backgrounds, although in the main they were not men who had experienced a sincere conversion to Islam. Some crossed over voluntarily, but many others originated as captives. Men taken in battle, seized in corsair raids, or picked up along the coast after shipwrecks had three options: ransom if they could afford it, slavery if they couldn't, or conversion if they wanted to make the best of a bad situation. Renegades were noticeable in the higher ranks of command in both the Moroccan and the Turkish militaries. Occasionally, unconverted Christians, whether prisoners of war or mercenaries, were also used, particularly for jobs requiring special skills.

For rank-and-file soldiery, the Andalusians, drawn from the refugee community of Iberian Muslims living in exile in Morocco, were considered the best troops. They were skillful in using the most advanced arms, and they were better trained, organized, and motivated than most native Moroccan troops. They were especially effective in fighting the Christians, against whom they felt an irreconcilable hatred. And well they should; the Andalusians in Abd al-Malik's army were the product of one of the most egregious examples of ethnic cleansing in early modern Europe.

During the long period when Christian and Muslim states shared the Iberian peninsula, both sides had generally tolerated members of the other religion as well as Jews, although this tended to be more true in Andalusia, the Muslim part of Iberia, than in the Christian states that eventually came together to form Spain. When Granada, the last Muslim state, surrendered to Spain in 1492, the peace terms included the promise of freedom of worship. Nevertheless, the government of a unified Christian Spain had no intention of allowing peaceful coexistence between religions. The bad news for Muslims came in two edicts, one in 1502 and the other in 1525, when the government reneged on its promise and ordered the conversion or expulsion of all Muslims.

Most Muslims chose conversion and became known as Moriscos. They accepted Christianity outwardly but retained their culture and social customs and married only within their own group. They were suspected, not without cause, of secretly practicing Islam. In 1567 hardliners on the Christian side moved to obliterate all traces of Islamic culture in Spain by regulating dress, dietary laws, language, even names. Morisco anger galvanized the following year in the War of Granada, a short, very nasty, and cruel guerilla war conducted largely in the Alpujarras Mountains. The Spanish army finally crushed the rebels in 1570, after which all Moriscos were first scattered around Spain, then, in 1609, expelled. Almost the entire population of Moriscos, estimated at between 275,000 and 300,000 men, women, and children, was rounded up and deported, mostly to North Africa. Spain's loss was North Africa's gain: The Andalusians, as the Moriscos became known, were a productive people who brought talent and skills to their adopted homelands. Those who became soldiers formed units under their own commanders. Although the full tragedy of the Moriscos had not yet been played out at the time Sebastian invaded Morocco, Andalusian refugees had been steadily swelling the armies of the sultan for some time.

Turks, Andalusians, and renegades, along with Arab and Berber tribesmen, headed toward the small spit of land extending from the top of the African continent on its northwestern side to meet the crusader king. The size of the Moroccan army that gathered under the Sa'dian white banners, gold-embossed with Qur'anic verses, to meet the Portuguese is uncertain. A contemporary English source, John Pory, reported forty thousand horse and eight thousand foot "besides Arabians and adventurers," but other Europeans put it as high as 120,000. Sebastian's own chief of staff mentions 40,000, which seems too low. Al-Zayyani gives a detailed breakdown of Abd al-Malik's army at the time he came to power: 14,000 Andalusians, 5,000 Berber tribesmen, 10,000 Arab tribesmen, 5,000 additional warriors from tribes that owed service to the dynasty, and an undetermined number of renegades and Turks. This must have swelled considerably once word of the invasion became known. Most other Moroccan sources do not provide figures but insist that the Portuguese force was larger, which it almost certainly was not. Modern estimates put the Moroccans at between sixty and seventy thousand.

While Sebastian waited, the Sa'di brothers marshaled their forces. Ahmad arrived leading troops from the Sus, only to find Abd al-Malik directing the casting of cannons. Ahmad then went on to Fez, where he took command of elite troops built around a corps of expert archers and a contingent of zealous disciples from a Sufi lodge. He is said to have been the first to arrive at the battle site picked by Abd al-Malik, although pinpointing Ahmad's exact location in the days leading up to the battle is problematic. In the sources he becomes ubiquitous, raising troops in one place, leading them in another, performing heroic acts in anticipation of the battle in still others. Sometime before the start of the battle—according to al-Zayyani, before the sultan left Marrakesh—Abd al-Malik fell seriously ill with symptoms that included fever, chills, and shaking. He had an unquenchable thirst but no appetite for food. He could sit on his horse for only short periods; mostly he had to be carried on a litter.

The Invasion

As the Moroccan army marched toward glory, Dom Sebastian waited. Contrary to his promise, Abd al-Malik never showed up. Instead he sent another letter that contained a taunt: "I will make a sixteen-day march to go to meet you, will you not make a single day's march to come to me?" Sebastian now decided it was time to get out of Arzila and head south to Larache. Several routes were considered, but Sebastian chose the one that lay inland, approaching Larache from the east, which required crossing several rivers and traveling through hostile territory cut off from the fleet. By far it was the most dangerous of the alternatives. Not surprisingly, Sebastian chose to show the king's flag in the teeth of the enemy. The Portuguese left Arzila on July 29. Waiting on the other side of the rivers, whose meandering courses formed a natural trap for an army coming from the north, was Abd al-Malik. He could scarcely believe his luck—or perhaps he could scarcely believe Sebastian's folly.

The march was a disaster. Trudging across Morocco under the summer sun in full battle dress weakened the Portuguese. The huge number of camp followers tagging along with the army included the wives and children of the soldiers, prostitutes, a thousand priests, and a stream of noblemen, the most important of whom rode in gilded coaches accompanied by their servants. Meanwhile the common soldier was having difficulty getting his basic rations. A Spanish report put the total size of the Portuguese procession at 46,000.

Sebastian's army moved slowly to the southeast across broken terrain until it approached the confluence of two rivers, the Wadi al-Makhazin and the Wadi Lukkus. These rivers were close enough to the sea to be tidal, and the Wadi al-Makhazin could be crossed at only one point when the tide was out, which the Portuguese did. Upstream, a bridge had been destroyed the night before in a daring raid by a cavalry detachment led by Ahmad. The Portuguese were now north of the town of Qasr al-Kabir, only a few miles from the ford across the Wadi Lukkus. This too could be crossed only at low tide; otherwise Sebastian was trapped in a cul-de-sac between the Wadi Lukkus and the Wadi al-Makhazin. The soldiers were exhausted from their six-day march over rough ground, the heat so intense their armor had to be cooled by pouring water on it. Standing between them and the Wadi Lukkus was the Moroccan army.

The battle was fought on August 4, 1578. From the very beginning, the two armies threw themselves upon each other, and for a while it was a slugfest, evenly fought but not between evenly matched sides. Hand-to-hand fighting is thirsty, exhausting work, and there was no break in the action. The Portuguese had no reserves, and their men were not rested when the battle began. The Moroccans, on the other hand, had reserves to back up their reserves—what must have seemed to the Portuguese an inexhaustible reservoir of men itching to join the fray. The two sides ground each other down until there was little left of the Portuguese.

Perhaps a master of tactics could have organized a retreat that would have saved part of the army. Dom Sebastian, however, had even less concept of tactics than of strategy, and while the battle raged, he made no pretense to command. His captains made their own tactical decisions, and each unit fought its own separate engagement. Sebastian was too busy scurrying back and forth with a small bodyguard of cavalrymen, shoring up the line wherever it sagged, stabbing and hacking at the enemy like a man possessed. This was the moment he had lived his whole life for, and he refused to be distracted from the noble task of individual combat by the practicalities of coordinating the ramshackle units of his army. At some point he must have wondered just when the skies would open and the heavenly host ride out to save the day. It never did. Thus Sebastian ensured that a disaster would become an annihilation.

On the Moroccan side, al-Fishtali and Ibn al-Qadi describe the battle largely in terms of what Ahmad did. Ahmad is simultaneously giving orders, leading countercharges, and fighting fiercely on the front line. Abd al-Malik, whose strategy had led the Portuguese into an almost impossible position and whose tactical decisions would carry the day, is conveniently ignored in these accounts. Ahmad did command a cavalry unit on the Moroccan right, and at the most dangerous point of the battle a Portuguese counterattack came in the vicinity of his command. Had the Moroccan force that faced this onslaught been shattered, a general rout could have followed. But the Moroccans held firm, and Ahmad is likely to have played an important role in this action. According to al-Fishtali, Ahmad had one horse shot out from under him, and he received a bullet wound in the chest, which somehow neither killed nor incapacitated him. The only explanation offered for this is that he was under the protection of God.

Sultan Abd al-Malik was dying when the battle began. At the moment of the Portuguese counterattack, he used his last strength to rise from his litter, mount his horse, and brandish his sword to rally his troops. The effort literally killed him, and upon returning to his litter, he died. Al-Ifrani maintains that his death was kept secret from all but his chief-of-staff, a renegade named Radwan; the sultan's Jewish physician; and the heir apparent, Ahmad. Radwan is said to have gone from tent to tent saying: "The sultan orders this one to go to this place, this one to stay near the flag, this one to go to the front, this one to go to the rear," and so forth. However, a Portuguese source, António de Saldanha, reports that the night before the battle, another renegade commander deserted to al-Mutawakkil carrying news that Abd al-Malik was near death and not expected to last until morning. A delighted al-Mutawakkil brought the renegade to Sebastian, but the Portuguese king considered the news to be "a great misfortune." Sebastian made no attempt to exploit the intelligence, and, as it turned out, the renegade's prognosis was somewhat premature. As usual, al-Mutawakkil had more insight into this matter than his noble Portuguese counterpart. Had Abd al-Malik's passing become known, some in his army would have lost heart and gone over to al-Mutawakkil, while many others would have lost their nerve and gone home. The death of Abd al-Malik represented the best chance the Portuguese had to win the battle.

Exactly what killed Abd al-Malik became a point of debate, his malady never having been diagnosed to everyone's satisfaction. Conventional thinking is that he died of natural causes, but in some Moroccan circles it was believed that he had been poisoned by Turkish officers on the orders of Radwan. According to this scenario, following the victory, the Turks intended to seize the country, but they decided against it in the face of the much larger Moroccan forces, who proclaimed Ahmad as sultan on the field of battle. If there is any truth to this, it was an ill-conceived plan because the new Moroccan king was much less beholden to the Turks and admired them far less than had Abd al-Malik. More likely the story of a Turkish assassination was a later Moroccan invention used to forfeit any sense of gratitude owed to a neighborhood bully who for once had lent a valuable hand.

The Consequences of Wadi al-Makhazin

If Abd al-Malik did not fall in battle, his nephew Muhammad al-Mutawakkil did, or rather he perished trying to escape across the river. His body was recovered, flayed, stuffed with straw, and paraded around the cities of Morocco as an object of derision. (Moroccan history often refers to him as Muhammad the Flayed.) Total casualties of the battle have been estimated at between seven and eight thousand on each side. In addition, the Moroccans took many prisoners, including a large number of noncombatants. A Moroccan report that is considered reasonable puts this number at about fourteen thousand. Philip II volunteered to serve as intermediary in ransoming the prisoners, and the Moroccans accepted his offer. Many of the poorer and less important captives would spend the rest of their lives as slaves in Morocco, but the families of the nobility paid to get their sons back.

Sebastian did not survive the slaughter he had caused. No one on the Portuguese side who saw Sebastian go down lived to tell about it, and apparently those who killed him had no idea who he was. After a three-day search, the sultan's officials found his body lying in the mud, looted and stripped, just another bloody, mangled corpse. The body was rumored to have been unceremoniously buried in an unmarked grave near Qasr al-Kabir, but according to the official report, it was dutifully turned over to Philip. One of the more ludicrous legacies of Sebastian's catastrophe was a cult popular in Portugal that insisted he was not really dead but in hiding and would return one day to lead Portugal back to greatness. This cult later took root in Brazil.

The defeat was an awful blow for a country the size of Portugal. On the casualty list were dukes, counts, bishops, and even a papal nuncio. Ransoming the living drained the country of its wealth. Most of Portugal's cash on hand plus valuables like precious stones passed into the coffers in Marrakesh. Portuguese prestige, already on the wane, plummeted abroad; never again would Lisbon be taken seriously as a major force in European power politics. The most drastic impact came in Portugal itself, where the throne passed to Sebastian's uncle, Cardinal Henrique,

Photo 2.3 The Death of Sebastian as envisioned by an eighteenth century artist. Courtesy of the Mary Evans Collection.

who had no heirs. Sebastian's cousin, Dom António, was illegitimate; the next in line was another uncle, none other than Philip II of Spain. By the time Henrique died in 1580, Philip's agents had spread enough money around Lisbon to smooth the way for a Spanish takeover. Philip's army marched in, Dom António escaped to exile in England, and Portugal disappeared for a while as an independent nation.

The Ottoman Empire, England, France, and the Dutch Republic all saw Wadi al-Makhazin as a blow against Iberian (by which they meant Spanish) power despite the fact that Spain gained the most from the Portuguese disaster. With the exception of France, they also interpreted it as a defeat of Catholicism, and in the Muslim world it was hailed as a victory of Islam over Christianity. Moroccan relations with England and France got better, and in London the Moroccan emissary was given such a warm reception that the Portuguese lodged an official protest. For Morocco the battle was a purely defensive victory; it gained much prestige but no land, nothing other than loot in the form of weapons, slaves, and ransom money. Wadi al-Makhazin did not make Morocco a great power. It meant only that, of the four states in the region, the weakest had prevented the next weakest from conquering it.

A CLOSER LOOK

The Battle of Wadi al-Makhazin

Having arrived first at the site of the battle, the Moroccans took the higher ground, with the sun to their backs. They deployed their arquebusiers in three long, crescent-shaped columns, Andalusians first, followed by renegades, then a mixture that included Turks, city militia, and men from the Sus. In front were thirty-four cannons, behind, a large square formed by the rest of the infantry. Cavalry flanked the columns and square, with spahis in the very front and the regular cavalry just behind. At the rear was a reserve force of light cavalry composed of tribesmen.

The Portuguese deployed in ten separate blocks around a hollow square. In the advance guard were regiments of the Adventurers, who were motivated if inexperienced. On the right were German mercenaries; on the left, the Spaniards and papal troops. Stretching behind each side were the main bodies of Portuguese infantry, and across the rear were the remaining Adventurers. Most of the artillery had been abandoned en route; the pieces that remained were positioned in front of the advance guard. In the hollow center of the square were the non-combatants. The Wadi Lukkus protected Sebastian's right, but his left was exposed and subject to sweeping cavalry charges. The woefully inadequate Portuguese cavalry was used to protect the flanks and artillery, but the larger portion of it was foolishly positioned on the cramped right rather than the exposed left. Al-Mutawakkil provided somewhat less than one thousand cavalry and about as many arquebusiers.

Tactical considerations were largely determined by the offensive and defensive positions of the respective forces. The Moroccan arquebusiers would keep pressure on the front while the cavalry pounded the Portuguese left until it pried the blocks apart and broke into the square. The best chance the Portuguese had was to keep their formation solid while inflicting so much damage on the attackers that they would abandon the field or rally to al-Mutawakkil. When enough attrition had occurred, the front-line regiments would slice through the crescents and strike a knockout blow at the center square.

The battle began in the morning with both sides firing their cannons without much effect. The Moroccan cavalry then penetrated the Portuguese flanks, disabling their artillery. Early on, the larger, more mobile Moroccan force was able to surround the Portuguese. The Portuguese counterattacked with pike and sword, breaking the Andalusians in the front line. Since the majority of the Moroccan troops consisted of horsemen, the most effective weapon on the Portuguese side should have been the pike, which could kill horse or rider. Tightly formed squares of pikemen had dominated European battlefields in the previous century, but not at Wadi al-Makhazin. There the spahis effectively neutralized the pikemen by using a tactic similar to one developed by companies of mounted pistoliers in Germany. This was a maneuver called the caracole, in which cavalrymen charged in ranks, each man firing his weapon in the face of the enemy before reeling around and clearing out to allow the next rank to follow. By the

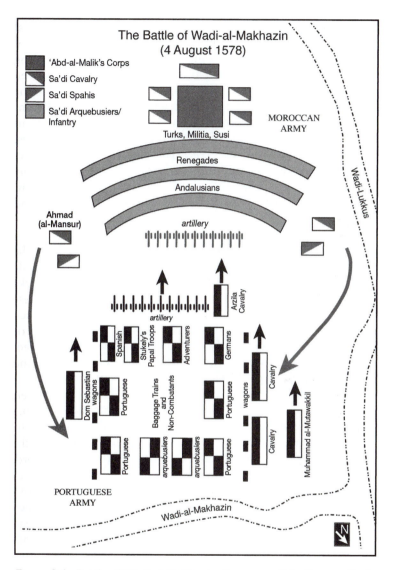

Figure 2.4   Battle of Wadi al-Makhazin. Courtesy of the Perseus Book Group.

time each rank had taken a turn, the first rank was reloaded and ready to go again.

Ultimately, the Portuguese front line led a second counterattack to punish the renegades who had moved up to take the place of the Andalusians. The Spanish and papal troops on the left, however, pushed forward too far, opening a gap between themselves and the block of conscripts protecting the left flank. Moroccan cavalry poured through this gap into the hollow square to attack from the rear. The square buckled: "The swords clashed and heaped blows of death," reports al-Ifrani, "until the moment when the wind of victory blew in favor of the Muslims. . . . Vanquished, the infidels turned their backs, but trapped in a circle of death they saw swords beating on their heads and when they wanted to take flight it was too late."

The square was shattered. The overextended unit of Spanish and Italians never made it back, disappearing in a sea of fluttering robes. Only a remnant of the Germans and some Portuguese cavalry held out. They were then obliterated by the entry of fresh troops, Arab horsemen who had been waiting to effect the coup de grace. Varying reports have the battle lasting between three and seven hours, with Ibn al-Qadi giving the specific figure of four hours and twenty minutes. Some of the broken pieces of the Portuguese army fell back, but there was no place to go. When they made for the river, they found the bridge destroyed. Even though the tide was at flood stage, many attempted to cross. Al-Zayyani claims that more Portuguese were drowned in the retreat than killed on the battlefield, further highlighting the exploits of Ahmad, the destroyer of the bridge. Other descriptions of the battle, however, make this unlikely. Only a handful of men from Sebastian's grand crusade straggled back to the coast, to be picked up by ships of the Portuguese fleet.

III

Al-Mansur Assumes Power

The task of steering Morocco through the breakers of international politics fell on Abd al-Malik's thirty-year-old brother, Abu l'Abbas Ahmad. He had become sultan in the most dramatic of ways: as the only surviving royalty on the field of battle. Surely this was a sign from God, not only that it was His will that Morocco remain part of the Land of Islam and that the Sa'dis continue to rule there, but also that this particular Sa'di had been divinely chosen. To celebrate the victory, Ahmad took the title al-Mansur bi Allah, "Victorious by the Will of God," and he is usually referred to simply as al-Mansur. If this was a bit presumptuous since the victory rightly belonged to Abd al-Malik, Morocco needed a live hero, and Ahmad was more than willing to play the role. Throughout his reign he would cultivate the image of the jihadist warrior even as he negotiated secret deals with Christian states and undermined fellow Muslims. In Ahmad al-Mansur the disconnect between ideology and action, which had first appeared during the reign of Muhammad al-Shaykh, now became manifest.

Al-Ifrani describes al-Mansur as "tall in height, with broad shoulders, full cheeks yellowish in color, brown hair and black eyes; he had well-set teeth and very brilliant incisors. His agreeable face was regular in shape." The Anonymous Chronicler of Fez provides a somewhat less dashing image: "His color was brown, his eyes deep-set in their sockets, and his beard thick: he had a scar on the left cheek; he was corpulent." Al-Fishtali assures his reader that his master was a man of "excellent appearance and beautiful attribute," a reflection of God's favor on him.

Al-Mansur's handsome physical appearance, as al-Fishtali saw it, matched the inner qualities with which the new sultan had been blessed. He was wise and knowledgeable, courageous yet patient, firm yet just, and above all pious. His lineage made him special: "No one can deny that there is not another ruler in the world to be so endowed"—a reference to Ahmad's direct descent from the Prophet Muhammad. Various saints, even the Prophet himself, it was said, had predicted the coming of Ahmad al-Mansur. Al-Ifrani skips the fawning, but he strongly implies that al-Mansur was the greatest of all Moroccan sultans. Even critical sources admit there was something exceptional about Ahmad al-Mansur. The Anonymous Chronicler of Fez thought the new sultan enjoyed a rare combination of insight and knowledge and was gifted with "the kindness of destiny," meaning that the fortuitous forces of the universe were aligned in him. He was a chosen one, although exactly what he was chosen to do would be a matter for interpretation.

Symbolizing Power: The Badi

If the chroniclers were not specific about what al-Mansur had been chosen for, al-Mansur himself had no doubt. He would lead his country and his dynasty to greatness; at this point, only God knew the specifics. He would begin in Marrakesh by continuing the work of al-Ghalib in making that city the splendid urban center it had been under earlier dynasties. He added buildings to the necropolis, the famous Sa'dian tombs that still grace Marrakesh. One interesting theory is that he used the Mamluk tombs of Cairo as his model, an indication that he had visited Egypt during those mysterious years of exile. He also began building a great mosque that was to be in the center of the city but was never finished. It stood on the spot that is today Marrakesh's most famous attraction, the bustling Jama al-Fna. He had a hospital established for Christian prisoners, and he completed a new Jewish quarter.

Marrakesh grew substantially from Andalusian and Jewish immigrants and from the many foreigners who poured in to serve the sultan and participate in the booming economy. Nor were his projects confined to Marrakesh. Outside the capital he constructed bridges and a major dam in the north, fortifications at Larache, and military towers on either side of Fez, a move that may have been designed more to control the population of that restive city than to protect it from siege. In Fez itself he added a great courtyard and fountain with a dome to the Qarawiyyin, the most splendid mosque in Morocco, and a library for the university it housed.

All other projects, however, paled when compared to the architectural wonder al-Mansur left as the capstone of his building program. After five months on the throne, he began the construction of a new palace in Marrakesh, dubbed al-Badi, "the Marvelous." The name was no exaggeration. Materials and men were brought in; hundreds of European architects, masons, artisans, and craftsmen were joined by thousands of exiled Andalusians and Iberian Jews who worked together for fifteen years on the project. The palace, which included more than five hundred columns, was constructed of black and white Italian marble obtained in direct trade, ton for ton, for Sus sugar. It had twenty domes and was square in design, with rooms facing an inner courtyard. The ceilings were painted in a riot of color, and gold was used to decorate ceilings and walls and to cover the cornices of the columns. Passages from the Qur'an and from court poets celebrating the magnificence of the palace's builder were inscribed on the walls, and flamboyant ceramic marquetry was used in the pavement. It was large enough to accommodate one thousand women. The building complex was surrounded by fountains and pavilions, and the outer grounds encompassed a huge area of citrus, palm, and olive groves as well as lush gardens. Streams of water flowed throughout the grounds and in and out of basins on both the lower and upper floors of the palace. Underground passageways were provided for servants so their comings and goings would not disturb the tranquility of the scene.

Of al-Badi, al-Ifrani notes: "It was a sort of terrestrial paradise, a marvel of the world, packed with art so that observers swooned with pleasure and admiration." António de Saldanha, who was a captive in Marrakesh for many years, described it as "the most grandiose palace that could be imagined" and "the most beautiful residence any king ever possessed." Others compared it to the old Umayyad palace at Cordoba or the Abbasid palace in Baghdad, two of the most glorious monuments in the Islamic world. The name itself was borrowed from one of the pavilions at Cordoba, and its design owed much to the Alhambra in Granada. The inspiration for al-Badi came from the past glories of Islam, particularly Andalusia, with little influence from styles then current in Europe or the Ottoman Empire. It made no attempt at innovation and did not so much as hint at a new idea. It was lavish, extravagant, sumptuous, and wildly pretentious. The man who lived in it was likened to the caliphs of old Baghdad, and European emissaries who visited him were dazzled. Seated on silk cushions piled on thick carpets with arabesque tapestries covering the walls and surrounded by bodyguards in colorful Turkish-style costumes, al-Mansur was the Western fantasy of an oriental potentate.

Al-Mansur did not wait until his palace was finished before moving in, but access to his living quarters was always carefully guarded. It was a capital crime punished by execution on the spot to be caught in the palace with anything that could be construed as a weapon. And if he occasionally allowed foreigners in so as to manipulate the image they were creating of him in the outside world, his personal life was not for public viewing. It was so carefully guarded that the names of his wives are different in al-Ifrani and António de Saldanha. One of the few peeks at his family life was given on a tour of his domain early in his reign when al-Mansur invited the Spanish ambassador into his tent. There the ambassador observed two of the sultan's "free" wives (who are described as "white and very beautiful"), three sons, and "a great number of young boys."

Consolidating Power: The Government

A magnificent palace and a revitalized capital were impressive symbols of power, but Ahmad al-Mansur was not satisfied with symbols. He would have real power, and he would always prefer the role of politician to that of soldier despite his martial title. Al-Ifrani calls him "a very able administrator; everything was firm and resolute in his plans." Some later historians hailed him as a man beyond his time, a visionary who was the first and, as it turned out, the only Moroccan ruler to conceive of a national policy before the twentieth century. Words like "modern" and "centralized," if not "Western," are used in describing his vision. He built a modern state from a messianic movement, and his policies laid the basis for the present-day nation of Morocco.

Other historians see Ahmad al-Mansur's vision as being like the architecture of al-Badi: more reactionary than futuristic, more traditional than innovative, more an attempt to resurrect the old than to embrace the new. They see a state based on religion-inspired models of the past rather than secular ones of the future. The model he used most was that of the Almohads of the twelfth and thirteenth centuries, the only previous Moroccan government that had attempted to transcend tribal society. The Almohads controlled a great empire extending eastward across the modern states of Algeria and Tunisia and northward to include much of Spain. Its founder, Ibn Tumart, based his authority on the claim that he was the Mahdi, and the propelling force binding the state was a zealous religious fundamentalism. The Almohad religious fervor had lasted about two generations, the state itself not much more than a century. Over the Almohad base al-Mansur draped Turkish trappings left over from Abd al-Malik's reign.

The only way to make sense of al-Mansur's life is to accept both visions. He was, above all else, an extraordinarily complex individual. Whichever concept was paramount at a given time, his achievements are apparent. He was a systematic organizer and planner who enjoyed an efficient administration by the standards of his time and an exceptionally efficient administration compared with other Moroccan governments. According to al-Fishtali, this was a result of his hard work and innate ability. To have a long-range impact, however, a ruler would need to establish institutions to carry his vision into the future. Otherwise a brilliant reign might turn out to be little more than a flash-in-the-pan.

For al-Mansur, communication was the key to successful governance. He was the great decision-maker, but he based his decisions on a steady stream of reports that poured in from officials across the realm. The sultan read these reports himself, and when appropriate he responded immediately. When he needed advice, he turned to the *diwan*, a weekly meeting of his council of ministers: high government officials, principal military advisers, and other notables. Those in attendance were expected to speak openly and honestly while the sultan listened. Then he made a decision, and the matter was settled. The diwan was served by a small army of lesser officials and secretaries. Ahmad al-Mansur was very much a hands-on ruler who took an interest in the daily running of affairs, even when addressing the everyday complaints of common subjects. Any man who had a grievance could petition the sultan directly after the midday Friday prayer, either at the tomb of his father or in an area of the Badi set aside for this purpose. Such complaints, often from those who believed they had been treated unjustly, were a high priority for any Muslim ruler because one of the fundamental charges for secular authority was to insure that all subjects were treated in a just manner. Sometimes these sessions would continue nonstop until the evening prayer.

If al-Mansur's government was efficient, it was also authoritarian. Al-Mansur made no pretense about this. His theory of politics, he once told the qadi of Fez who had reproached him for his oppressive policies, was based on the assumption that "the people of Morocco are madmen whose madness can be treated only by keeping them in chains and iron collars." His system was based strictly on the concept of one-man rule. Nor was al-Mansur's government in any way open. In his obsession with cloak and dagger, the sultan created his own secret code for writing dispatches. It consisted of characters he invented, which he then mixed with Arabic letters to make the text indecipherable to all except his sons, his highest officials, and his most faithful servants. Al-Fishtali thought the code extremely clever and said so in his book, which made its existence less secret. If al-Mansur's behavior in this matter appears peculiar, he did have reason for concern. Some of his rivals on the international scene, particularly Spain and the Ottoman Empire, had good spy and information-gathering networks within Morocco. So al-Mansur developed his own espionage system to keep himself informed of potential troublemakers within his realm and of what was going on in Madrid, Granada, and Algiers.

The new sultan needed as much intelligence as he could get during the first years of his reign, when conditions were unsettled and rivals tested his mettle. Some Turkish officials had been contemplating a move against Abd al-Malik before Sebastian preempted them, and al-Mansur was far less their man than Abd al-Malik was supposed to have been. According to the Anonymous Chronicler of Fez, following the Battle of Wadi al-Makhazin, Ahmad had to flee for fear the Turks would kill him and enthrone a compliant son of Abd al-Malik. The people of Marrakesh insisted on Ahmad, however, and the Turks backed off (all of which fits rather nicely into the theory that Abd al-Malik was assassinated). If no hard evidence exists to support the contention that the Turks were plotting to take over Morocco on the heels of the Battle of Wadi al-Makhazin, real threats in which the Turks seem to have played a role would soon materialize. In some murky doings, al-Mansur managed to purge several of Abd al-Malik's top generals, including Radwan, the chief-of-staff at Wadi al-Makhazin.

A somewhat clearer incident involved the chief qa'ids (commanders) of the Andalusians led by Sa'id al-Dughali. Both António de Saldanha and al-Fishtali report that al-Mansur's distrust of the Andalusians began at the time al-Dughali betrayed al-Mutawakkil and went over to Abd al-Malik. During Sebastian's invasion, according to al-Fishtali, Ahmad kept a spy on al-Dughali, fearing he could be bought by anyone, even invading Christians, so long as the price was right. António de Saldanha sees a broader perspective, no less than an attempt by the Andalusians to seize the country and make it their own. The Andalusians fought for Morocco at Wadi al-Makhazin, but soon thereafter, in the al-Fishtali account, al-Dughali tried to slip away to the Sus, where his men were organizing an army to march on Marrakesh and Fez, apparently to make al-Dughali the sultan. Al-Mansur, however, was keen to their subterfuge and sent a detachment of men loyal to himself, who caught up to al-Dughali and dispatched him and his chief henchmen. For António de Saldanha, the last straw came when al-Mansur discovered the Andalusian qa'ids embezzling Portuguese ransom money. He invited them to his palace, where he had their heads cut off.

In July 1581 al-Mansur decided he needed to make some arrangement for the royal succession, and he announced that his oldest son, Muhammad al-Shaykh al-Ma'mun, would be next in line for the throne. This sparked a rebellion led by al-Mansur's nephew, Dawud b. Abd al-Mu'min, who claimed that under the Sa'di system the oldest member of the next generation, namely himself, was the legitimate successor. Dawud received some assistance from the Turks in Algiers but was defeated and driven off. For a while at least, subsequent rebellions had more to do with taxation than succession, and court chroniclers made no attempt to hush them up. Such outbreaks were attributed more to the natural unruliness of the Berbers than to the misrule of Ahmad al-Mansur. Indeed, al-Mansur was more often praised for his strong and what may appear harsh treatment of recalcitrants than criticized for a lack of compassion or forbearance.

Perhaps the most notorious instance of al-Mansur's calculated, cold-hearted wrath involved the Zuwawa. They were tribesmen whose homeland was between Algiers and Tlemcen and who often served the Turks as mercenaries. An army of about 10,000 of them stayed behind in Morocco after Wadi al-Makhazin, but their chiefs became disgruntled and secretly decided to recognize an alternative sharif as sultan. Al-Mansur, however, got word of this. He announced a general payday to take place in the palace. One by one the Zuwawa marched into one door of the palace, were paid, and as they exited through another door, had their throats cut until a reported 8,000 of them lay dead.

Although al-Mansur suffered the usual problems a sultan was likely to face if he expected his people to obey orders and pay their taxes, his position on the throne was more secure than that of any other ruler in his dynasty. At a glance, the system of government that began with Muhammad al-Shaykh and culminated under Ahmad al-Mansur appears similar to the absolutist monarchies then taking shape in Europe. A deeper look, however, reveals profound differences in such basic matters as social structure, fiscal policy, and the relationship between religion and politics. And in Morocco there was an alarming gulf between state and society. In a sense, al-Mansur's government was too cosmopolitan for its time. Al-Fishtali notes that Moroccans had taken offense at many of the foreign influences introduced by Abd al-Malik and that al-Mansur had eliminated them. If al-Mansur did purge many foreign influences, he did not get rid of the foreigners themselves; he employed many renegades,

Andalusians, Turks, Iberian Jews, and Europeans-for-hire in all the higher slots of the central government. This professed jihadist warrior even allowed Roman Catholic priests to establish a church in Marrakesh, with the one proviso that they could not ring a bell to call their parishioners to worship. And while the *diwan* appeared to assist the sultan in governing the realm, al-Mansur may have sought economic advice on such crucial matters as the sugar industry and trans-Saharan trade from a secretive shadow cabinet made up of Jewish businessmen. They worked to strengthen the power of a state and a dynasty that had protected and supported them and under which they had prospered.

Drawing talent from across the board seems to have made more sense than designating by birth a small group to serve as a ruling class, as was the practice in much of Europe. But it meant that al-Mansur's government was imposed on native Moroccans rather than having grown out of them, making the state independent of the society it ruled. And the society itself remained fragmented into separate and often conflicting ethnic, cultural, social, and economic groups. The state would not become an agent for homogenizing the society, as would happen in many places in Europe.

Enforcing Power: The Army

A state apparatus with an effective bureaucracy would administer power for al-Mansur, but to make that arrangement work, he needed an irresistible force to impose his will. The Moroccan military had been in the process of reorganization since the time of Muhammad al-Shaykh; if it had not changed, Morocco would not have survived. The traditional view is that the Moroccan army became steadily Ottomanized in the period from Muhammad al-Shaykh to Ahmad al-Mansur. The Ottomans had an effective modern military that was also Muslim, making it the ideal model for the Sa'dis. According to al-Fishtali, however, under Muhammad al-Shaykh, al-Ghalib, and al-Mutawakkil, the army remained organized along traditional lines, "Arab fashion"; Abd al-Malik introduced the "Turkish system," and al-Mansur combined the two.

Certainly Turkish influence peaked under Abd al-Malik. Abd
al-Malik had not only seen top-of-the-line Ottoman troops in
his years of exile, he had commanded them. Even al-Mansur
had to admit, if grudgingly, that the Turkish contingents at
Wadi al-Makhazin had been among the best equipped, organized, trained, and disciplined on either side of the field. But
much of the Ottomanization process that took place in Abd
al-Malik's two years on the throne was superficial, such as having
his men parade around in flashy Turkish uniforms. Substantial
elements were introduced on the organizational level, including
Turkish titles and ranks from pasha on down, and Turks and
renegades—many of the Turks who served in Morocco were by
origin renegades, or "Turks by convenience"—acted as advisers
and instructors. According to one estimate, there were about
2,000 Turks in the Moroccan army. Nevertheless, the modern-
ization of the Moroccan army appears to have developed more
as a result of Andalusian than Turkish influence. Even though
the Andalusians had lost their war against the Spanish, they had
been on the cutting edge of European military technology and
tactics for some time.

The Andalusians so dominated the Moroccan army that they
were themselves divided into units based on where in Spain
their families had originated and where in Morocco they currently resided. Al-Mansur, however, never forgot the spectre of
al-Dughali and an Andalusian Kingdom of Morocco. As a result,
the highest positions in his army were mostly occupied by renegades. António de Saldanha called the Moroccan army under
al-Mansur "the most brillant ever seen in Barbary," but he believed it was too big for the country it served. A major theme in
his work is that al-Mansur could not afford his own army,
which was always in danger of becoming a force unto itself.

Al-Mansur had under his direct command an army of fifty
thousand, the core of which was sixteen thousand professionals
in Marrakesh and ten thousand in Fez. They were paid on a regular basis monthly or quarterly. To a large extent, rank was based
on merit. Scattered around the rest of the country, al-Mansur's
sons commanded their own armies, each stationed in a particular city, with the crown prince residing in Fez. Military units
were divided by ethnicity, function, and region: for example,

Andalusian musketeers, renegade artillerymen, Sussi cavalrymen, Turkish spahis.

Complementing the professionals was the traditional side of the army made up of tribal warriors, city militias, disciples from the militant *zawiyas,* and various volunteers in time of need. The Sa'dis added new tribes to the privileged groups that provided military service in lieu of paying taxes. Even if they were not up to par with the professional troops, the traditional groups allowed the sultan to assemble an enormous amount of manpower, as had been done at Wadi al-Makhazin. And they could be used to balance the professional sector should the professionals get ideas about assuming power for themselves (a chronic problem in Algiers). Had the tribesmen been simply cut loose, pushed out from under the tent of the sultan, so to speak, some would likely have ended up as independent forces, rebels, or brigands.

The Sa'dis had always believed in the large-scale use of firearms. Al-Mansur inherited an arsenal of European-made weapons left by the Portuguese on the field at Wadi al-Makhazin, and by his time the Moroccan arms manufacturing industry was well established, producing both cannons and muskets. But al-Mansur's needs soon outran his sources of supply, and he turned to imports from England. Although there was no immediate threat on the horizon, he increased his purchases to the point that the English had to cut back in order to prepare for their own imminent showdown with Spain in 1588.

Dealing with Power: The Ottomans and Spain

A victorious army backed by a powerful government might tempt a man like Ahmad al-Mansur to undertake rash deeds. An attempt to expand to the north or east would run into one of the superpowers, however, and that would be an act more suicidal than aggressive. Not that al-Mansur backed away from the sort of diplomatic maneuver the Sa'dis loved so well (although the example of his father's assassination was always before him). In any case, the world of 1580 had become too dangerous.

On his accession to power following the Battle of Wadi al-Makhazin, Ahmad al-Mansur received embassies in Marrakesh from all the major European and Islamic powers, who congratulated him and brought gifts. Delegations from England, France, and the Dutch Republic arrived, as did one from a chastened Portugal that consisted of ornate chariots laden with silver, beautiful vases, and other precious objects. But it was Philip II of Spain's offering that stole the show. The Spanish delegation consisted of forty persons bearing gifts that were considered to be "great" even by Mustafa al-Jannabi. They included four (or forty; the reference is vague) boxes of pearls that were poured out under the eyes of al-Mansur. Fewer in number but equally startling were the precious gems, huge sapphires removed from the crown of Philip's father (according to al-Ifrani), along with unspecified "luxurious curiosities" and even some weapons.

That al-Mansur welcomed ambassadors from both the Ottoman Empire and Spain at the same time—thereby announcing his intention to maintain good relations with both—must have been a great disappointment to the Turks, given their recent assistance and the Spanish support for the Portuguese. Following the Battle of Wadi al-Makhazin, the Ottoman sultan, Murad III, sent a letter to al-Mansur, ostensibly to congratulate him on his victory. Murad used such words as "mighty," "radiant," and "dazzling" to describe his own domain and referred to himself as "master over the kings of both East and West." The sense of the Turkish message was that the Sa'dis could enjoy autonomy, but they had to acknowledge the sultan in Constantinople as supreme leader of the Islamic world.

The Ottoman embassy presented its gifts just before the Spanish. They consisted of a robe of honor, a turban, a sword and other arms inlaid with gold, and a signet ring, all typical offerings one Muslim ruler might present to another, in some cases from one of a more exalted rank to one of a somewhat lower or subordinate rank. Al-Mansur was most impressed by the sword, which had a blade of steel so pure it was said that nothing like it had ever been seen in Morocco. Nevertheless, the Ottoman gifts were very modest when compared to those of the Spanish. Al-Mansur, according to al-Jannabi, turned to the Ottoman ambassador for an explanation. He was told: "These gifts are on his [Murad III's] part a mark of friendship and welcome, because you are Sharif and practice jihad." The Spanish envoys "on the contrary come only to court you." The Ottoman sultan, al-Mansur was reminded, was above all kings and was not afraid of anyone; rather, everyone was afraid of him. To this, al-Mansur replied, "Without doubt he is our great chief and the most distinguished among us; his glory raises him above the other kings," again, as reported by al-Jannabi.

Whatever al-Mansur actually muttered—and although al-Jannabi was not present at those proceedings, he had access to the Ottoman representatives who were—the affair apparently did not sit well with either al-Mansur or the Turks. For the next three years the Turks saw the Moroccans tilting ever in the direction of Spain and concluded that the young sultan had been awed by Philip's ostentatious gifts. But the Turks underestimated al-Mansur: He would not be the kind of king who would make a foreign policy based on boxes of pearls. He did become increasingly chummy with the Iberian Christians, but the responsibility for this is a matter of interpretation. In one scenario al-Mansur came to the throne sharing his father's dislike of the Turks despite the hospitality they had showed him during his period of exile and the help they had accorded at the Battle of Wadi al-Makhazin. He once referred to them as "a group of slaves and lackeys whom God had imposed on the Muslims." This theme was elaborated on by al-Mansur's ambassador to Constantinople, who equated the Ottomans with the Mamluks of Egypt, that is, very high ranking slaves or "proxies for those who are more entitled and qualified for such power and authority," meaning, of course, the direct descendants of Muhammad.

According to a different scenario, al-Mansur was willing to play a role similar to the one Abd al-Malik had played, or was supposed to have been playing. However, Turkish machinations from the onset of his reign, including assassination plots, attempted coups, and support for rivals, soured him. He could only conclude that the Ottomans preferred some other candidate for the throne in Marrakesh, and he was not going to accede to this. In fact, the Turks did keep a son of Abd al-Malik named Ismail in Algiers just in case a switch of rulers became necessary. According to António de Saldanha, emissaries sent by al-Mansur to bring gifts to the Turkish leaders in Algiers attempted to poison Ismail while they were in town. The plot failed only because the concubine they had bribed to carry out the deed lost her nerve at the last moment.

Soon after al-Mansur came to power, the Ottoman sultan's name was dropped from the Friday prayer, and the tribute and gifts that had once flowed to Constantinople dried up. According to the Anonymous Chronicler of Fez, a secret agreement was made with Philip II in which the Moroccans promised not to attack Spanish outposts on the Mediterranean coast. Further negotiations led to a proposed pact of twenty years' duration under which the Spanish promised to come to the aid of Morocco in case of an Ottoman attack, and in return Morocco would hand Larache over to the Spanish. In the summer of 1580 al-Mansur provided Madrid with a gesture of his good faith. Moriscos in Seville had been plotting to raise another revolt in league with supporters in Morocco, through whom al-Mansur learned of the matter. He passed this information on to the Spanish, and the plot was quashed. The following year he revived one of his father's old schemes, a combined Spanish-Moroccan invasion of the regency of Algiers, with which he teased Philip.

Somewhere along the line Ahmad al-Mansur overstepped his bounds. Unlike Abd al-Malik, al-Mansur had not developed personal ties with officials in Algiers, chief among whom was a vigorous and capable kapudan pasha (supreme admiral) named Uluj Ali. This official had been instrumental in the decision to assist Abd al-Malik, but he had taken a dislike to al-Mansur. Uluj Ali had come to the conclusion that Morocco would be an excellent base from which to carry the holy war into the Atlantic and perhaps launch an invasion of Granada.

In 1581 the kapudan pasha was able to use a careless insult by Ahmad al-Mansur in not responding to a letter from Murad III to convince his master that it was time for another invasion of Morocco. Al-Mansur got word of this and hastily dispatched an embassy to Constantinople. The Moroccans were able to mollify the Ottomans, but only after eating a bitter slice of humble pie. The invasion fleet was cancelled virtually on the point of sailing, and the following year Uluj Ali was transferred to another part of the empire.

The near disaster of 1581 had a sobering effect on Ahmad al-Mansur, who henceforth tended to show more deference toward the Ottoman sultan. The Moroccans paid a tribute of over 100,000 gold coins and in outward appearance agreed to show official respect to the Ottoman ruler. In return they were unofficially left alone. Al-Mansur and Murad III carried on a correspondence in which the Moroccan sultan was always polite and complimentary, referring to the Ottoman Empire as "glorious" and its dynasty as "exalted." Murad himself was the recipient of a long list of flattering terms from "monumental" to "unique," although it is interesting to note that al-Mansur's correspondence with Elizabeth of England and Philip II of Spain praised them with flattery as well. Al-Mansur referred to the unity and the "love" between the Ottoman and Sa'di governments, with the implication that this relationship was between equals, a nuance not evident in Murad's letters. Al-Mansur also frequently reminded his Turkish counterpart of the importance of a sharifian lineage.

Morocco's basic problem, al-Mansur came to realize, was more with Algiers than with Constantinople, at least where military and political issues were concerned. Ideological issues were a separate category over which the Sa'dis and Ottomans would remain at odds, but they were not likely to lead to war. For Marrakesh, maintaining civil relations with Constantinople was necessary in the hope that the Ottomans would rein in Algiers. A faction in the Ottoman court continued to advocate the creation of a huge fleet to sail across the Mediterranean, reasserting Turkish power in the sometimes independent-minded regencies of Algiers, Tunis, and Tripoli, and conquering Morocco once and for all. This party, however, did not prevail against other factions that wanted to attack Persia in one direction or Austria in the other. As for the garrison in Algiers, it lost much of its aggressive spirit after the departure of Uluj Ali. In the following decade the pendulum swung the other way as the Turks began to fear al-Mansur's influence among disaffected groups in their own territory, particularly in the *zawiyas*.

Although the Spanish and the Ottomans vied for prestige and power in Marrakesh during the first years of Ahmad al-Mansur's reign, the new sultan could not have guessed that the Mediterranean powder keg was about to be defused. In 1578 Spanish ambassadors had arrived in Constantinople to begin secret negotiations. The Portuguese invasion of Morocco added an unwanted complication, but once Sebastian was safely dead and his army annihilated, the talks proceeded. After seven decades of battering each other, the two empires had exhausted themselves, and in August 1580 Spain and the Ottoman Empire concluded a truce in which they agreed not to attack each other. While this was never officially recognized as a peace, over the succeeding years it became one. Despite minor violations, the two states never returned to full-scale warfare, which meant that the status quo of 1580 held. North Africa remained solidly Muslim, but Andalusia was lost forever. The Turks maintained a presence in the Western Mediterranean as far as Algiers, but henceforth they would present no threat to Spain.

For Morocco, the long-range impact of the Spanish-Ottoman truce would be profound and not altogether positive. For the time being, however, it allowed al-Mansur considerable latitude in playing the big power game, particularly after Uluj Ali was recalled and something of a détente was reached with Constantinople. With the Ottomans no longer threatening invasion, the treaty al-Mansur's representatives had so carefully negotiated with the Spanish was put into limbo. This was much to the chagrin of Philip, who wanted Larache for a naval base to protect his shipping from pirates of two varieties, Barbary in the Mediterranean and English, Dutch, and French in the Atlantic. Philip had his own Moroccan pretenders waiting in the wings, including a son of al-Ghalib and a son of al-Mutawakkil. At one time he considered seizing the city by force, but his more cautious side prevailed. He continued to negotiate with al-Mansur, who never completely turned him down but engaged in a masterful game of stalling that lasted more than three years, after which the issue faded.

Manipulating Power: Playing the English Card

The Spanish had to be careful in dealing with Morocco, even after Spain's disengagement from the Ottoman Empire. Too much Spanish pressure could strengthen al-Mansur's tie with England at a time when Spain and England were moving toward the collision that came in 1588 with the Spanish Armada.

Al-Mansur, like his father, had no intention of aligning Morocco too closely with Spain, which ideologically was supposed to be the enemy. If the Spanish were useful against the Turks, the English were useful against the Spanish. Al-Mansur hoped the Protestant powers led by England would help him resurrect Andalusia. And there were those in the English government who had convinced themselves that Protestantism and Islam shared a purer sense of monotheism than what they considered the saint-ridden idolatry of Roman Catholicism and thus were ideological allies. English public opinion paid considerable attention to Morocco as details of the Battle of Wadi al-Makhazin became available. The English were especially interested in the role played by their rogue countryman, Thomas Stukeley, who had died fighting alongside his Italian condottieri. A popular play, *The Battle of Alcazar*, had Stukeley as its main character. Al-Mansur himself is reflected in two plays of Shakespeare, as the Prince of Morocco in *The Merchant of Venice*, who chooses the wrong casket and loses the heiress, and in the composite character of Othello, the romantic, heroic, and very vulnerable Moorish general.

Queen Elizabeth, however, could not deal openly with al-Mansur. Some Catholics had found it convenient to blame England for the Portuguese catastrophe on the ground that the English had armed the soldiers who had shed so much Christian blood. Of Elizabeth, the papal nuncio in Spain complained: "There is no evil that is not devised by that woman, who, it is perfectly plain, succoured Molucco [Abd al-Malik] with arms, and especially with artillery." The Virgin Queen still had Roman Catholics at home to worry about, and she did not want to antagonize the Papacy, which had forbidden trading arms with Morocco.

English policy toward Morocco during the 1580s revolved around one central issue. The English were determined to cause trouble for Spain in Portugal by supporting the claims of the pretender Dom António, and they tried doggedly to enlist Morocco as an ally. If Portugal could be retaken, Spain would be surrounded and eventually crushed. Al-Mansur could not have cared less about the fortunes of Dom António, the last scion of the hated House of Avis that had caused so much trouble for Morocco, but supporting his cause allowed Marrakesh to draw closer to London. Following the defeat of the Spanish Armada, the English decided to take the offensive with their own invasion of Portugal.

Al-Mansur sent a delegation to London in January 1589 to coordinate support for this action. Among the various items of discussion that were bandied about was a Moroccan proposal for the English to send al-Mansur one hundred ships, which he would fill with fighting men for the invasion of Portugal, and he would provide a subsidy of 150,000 gold coins. He also wanted a treaty that would later allow him to hire English ships to fight against unnamed non-Christian enemies—in other words, the Turks. To the English, there was no doubt that the Moroccans committed themselves to an English-led attack. However, when it came the following June, the Moroccans were nowhere to be seen, and for various reasons the entire operation turned out to be a disaster.

In fact, al-Mansur had neither suitable troops to fill one hundred English ships nor the money, either for the subsidy or for the hiring of English ships. Had Elizabeth gone along with his scheme to reintroduce Islam into Western Europe, England would have become a pariah in the Christian community, so negotiations on those matters stalled. Throughout the period of Anglo-Moroccan rapprochement, al-Mansur maintained cordial relations with Spain and an unofficial alliance against the Ottomans. The English were even more duplicitous; desperate to break the Spanish-Ottoman truce, they indicated to Constantinople their willingness to support a Turkish takeover of Morocco so that the Ottomans would have a base for raiding Spanish shipping in the Atlantic.

Not surprisingly, relations between England and Morocco cooled. The English accused al-Mansur of bad faith in the Portuguese debacle, and he responded that because they had not kept him informed of the precise date of the attack, it was all their fault. Then, a few months later, a curious situation arose. On the night of September 23, 1589, the Spanish evacuated the old Portuguese fort of Arzila, Sebastian's take-off point for his fateful march, and the Moroccans quickly occupied it. The official Moroccan explanation was that Philip had ordered this because he feared the might of al-Mansur. In fact, Philip's spies

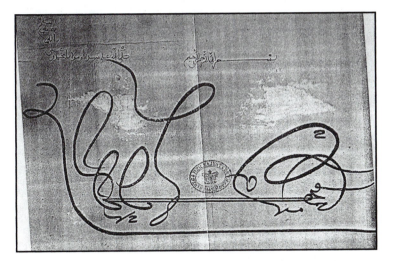

Figure 3.1   Al-Mansur's signature. Courtesy of Batchworth Press, 1952.

had kept him informed about Anglo-Moroccan negotiations over the invasion of Portugal, so he opened his own negotiations with al-Mansur. Thus, at the same time al-Mansur was striking a deal to assist the English in invading Portugal, he was making an even more secret deal with the Spanish to double-cross the English in return for Arzila.

Ibn al-Qadi noted that al-Mansur's greatness was recognized "among councils in the lands of the unbelieving enemy. . . . Even though he is an enemy to them, they honor him and laud the character qualities that God has granted to him." After more than a decade of dealing with al-Mansur, however, the English were hardly lauding his character qualities any more than were the arch unbelieving enemy, the Spanish. On al-Mansur's side, he appears oblivious to any hint that his word was no longer considered his bond. His relationship with England continued to be full of grand schemes in support of Dom António, aimed against the Spanish with the intention of keeping the English from turning to the Ottomans.

Al-Mansur spent much diplomatic energy reassuring his potential friends and enemies: reassuring the English that he was really on their side against Spain, reassuring the Spanish that he was really on their side against the Ottoman Empire (and that he wasn't on England's side), and reassuring the Turks that he was really on their side against the Spanish and the rest of Christendom. His tactics included protestations of friendship, vague proposals for alliances, and protracted negotiations that never delivered concrete results. To a large extent, he got away with this because once the Portuguese were out of the picture, everyone he dealt with had a more inveterate enemy elsewhere and hoped to use Morocco against that enemy. That this never happened was due to the genius of Ahmad al-Mansur.

IV

Commander of the Faithful

For Ahmad al-Mansur, religion was the very foundation of life.
If in his daily doings he had to kill, plunder, lie, and commit
other acts that appeared morally unacceptable, he showed no
sign of remorse or guilt, nor did such behavior ever shake his
religious beliefs. António de Saldanha characterizes al-Mansur
as being more superstitious than devout, or, as he put it, the sultan was "addicted to sorcery." In making important decisions,
he frequently followed the advice of "magicians" and relied
heavily on astrology. António de Saldanha had little understanding of Islam, and, in any case, the line between supersition
and religion, whether Christianity or Islam, was easily crossed
in the sixteenth century. Al-Fishtali emphasizes the sultan's
piety: Sometimes he stayed up all night to pray, and he was devoted to the practice of visiting the tombs of saints and other
holy places to accumulate *baraka*. From a modern perspective,
the sultan's zealousness and attention to his faith should not be
seen as contrived. He was said to be devoted to knowledge,
which in the context of his time meant religious study. He knew
the Qur'an and the *hadith* (sayings attributed to the Prophet),
and he corresponded with scholars from as far away as Egypt.
In his own land he subsidized scholars and encouraged promising
students to embark on academic careers. He sought out living
saints and noted jurisconsults, and he honored them with personal audiences. He himself was hailed as a living saint blessed

with the bloodlines of the Prophet and the *baraka* he had accumulated through his own actions.

Taming the Religious Establishment

The religious establishment was another matter. Al-Mansur considered it to be essentially political in nature, which led him to distrust it. In his mind, religious leaders were quick to criticize or to offer unwanted advice, but they had little appreciation of the practicalities involved in operating a government and no understanding of state policy. When his army caught two marabouts who had been stirring up tribesmen against the sugar industry, al-Mansur ordered them to be flayed alive. The Sa'dis did not prove to be eternally grateful to those who had promoted their cause during their rise to power, and they had no interest in sharing power with former allies. Elements of the religious establishment had joined the tax rebellions against Muhammad al-Shaykh, and he had repressed them with a vengeance. In 1547 he invited the heads of some of the more troublesome *zawiyas* to Marrakesh and had them massacred. Seven years later he came down on the Sufi brotherhoods of Fez, plundering their property, closing their *zawiyas*, and dispersing their disciples.

The Jazuliyya Sufi order was a particular problem because its support had been crucial in the Sa'di struggle against the Wattasids, and its ideology had smoothed the way for a sharifian dynasty to take power. Nevertheless, Jazulite ideology was revolutionary and promoted political activism. Although the Jazuliyya did not aim to assume direct power, its leaders in their role as guardians of moral Islam did expect to guide, and when necessary to criticize, those who were in power. The Sa'dis, who had no intention of being guided or criticized, feared that sooner or later a *qutb* would emerge from the Jazuliyya to challenge royal authority. Nor were the Sa'dis inclined to allow the *zawiyas* to remain autonomous, as many had been during the period when the central government was weak. Muhammad al-Shaykh had purged one faction of the Jazuliyya he thought the most dangerous, executing or driving its leadership into exile, and Ahmad al-Mansur would keep a steady rein on the surviving factions.

Sufi lodges and rural marabouts were not the only components of the religious establishment that concerned the Sa'dis. The ulama, the class of scholars and judges who congregated in urban areas, were supposed to participate in the selection of a secular ruler and make sure he guided the state according to the strict dictates of Islamic law. Again, in theory, the ulama were expected to offer advice, solicited or not, and to render criticism when laws were transgressed or the ruler behaved in an unjust manner. At most times and in most places in the Islamic world, rulers did not welcome such oversight, and most members of the ulama did not interfere in matters that could bring the secular authority down on them. The Sa'dis began their rule with a special distrust of the ulama of Fez, which had sided with the Wattasids during the civil war and already had a list of martyrs. Al-Mansur had no compunction about adding to it when necessary.

Connected to the ulama of Fez was a local *shurafa* family, the Idrisids, whose ancestors had founded the city and once ruled over a state in the northern part of the country. The Idrisids were rich and locally powerful, but they were not natural allies of the Sa'dis, whom they considered rustic upstarts of suspect genealogy. Ahmad al-Mansur would have occasion to deal with these distant relatives later in his reign. Although he seems to have spent considerable time in Fez during his youth, there are indications that he never felt comfortable there once he came to power. He did not often visit Fez, and when there he preferred to hold court on its outskirts. He encouraged members of the Fezi ulama whom he favored to relocate in Marrakesh.

The Caliphate

Ahmad al-Mansur claimed to have had a dream in his youth in which he saw the Prophet Muhammad surrounded by a brilliant light: "The idea came to me," he said, "of consulting him on the chance that I had to gain supreme power. Knowing my thought immediately, the Prophet responded to it in a precise fashion, because with three of his noble fingers, the thumb, the index and the middle together, he made a gesture toward me saying: 'Commander of the Faithful.'" This was a caliphal title that by the sixteenth century was rarely used even by the Ottoman sultan. Al-Mansur understood that the fingers held up by the Prophet represented the age at which he would assume caliphal responsibilities, each finger representing a decade of his life. Ahmad was thirty when he took the throne, meaning that he would become caliph at the moment he became ruler of Morocco. He was already *sharif* and sultan, but those were pedestrian titles by comparison. As caliph he was leader of all Muslims in the world, and in theory all the lands of Islam were under his authority; it was his duty to unite all Muslims and to use whatever means necessary to defend Islam.

The word "caliph" (from *khalifa*, deputy or steward) came to mean successor to the Prophet Muhammad as political and military leader of the Muslim community. Although it was not originally intended as a spiritual office, it subsequently took on religious connotations. The caliph came to be viewed as God's representative among men; his role was to lead the community of believers in a proper manner as specified by the holy writs of Islam. He was originally chosen by consensus, actually by a council of notables; at least the first four caliphs following the death of Muhammad were selected in this way, with the proviso that every caliph had to come from the Prophet's tribe, the Quraysh. The caliph's position was given legitimacy only after the ulama had taken an oath of allegiance to him known as the *bay'a*. In return, the caliph had to promise to rule justly, which meant in accordance with Islamic law. Once this was done, the community was obligated to obey the caliph under all conditions.

In 661 the caliphate became a hereditary monarchy, at first under the Umayyad dynasty of Damascus and later under the Abbasids of Baghdad. Over the centuries the caliphs gradually saw their religious prerogatives diffuse to the ulama and other groups like the *shurafa* and Sufi orders and their political power give way to the sultans, who were more like temporal kings ruling over separate territories. Sometimes sultans claimed the title of caliph, but there was supposed to be only one caliph in the world, while there could be many sultans. In the tenth century rival caliphates emerged, the first one in Andalusia, with its capital at Cordoba, and then another in Egypt. In the thirteenth century the caliphate in Baghdad was destroyed by the Mongols; although a member of the Abbasid family relocated in Cairo, henceforth the caliphs were puppets of the Mamluks, who ruled Egypt until the Ottomans conquered it in 1517.

In most of the Islamic world the ideal of a universal caliphate died somewhere between the tenth and sixteenth centuries. The idea of the caliphate, however, was implicit in the Sa'di movement from the beginning, and the fear that Muhammad al-Shaykh would use it to challenge the Ottoman claim of supremacy over the Muslim world was a consideration in the Turkish decision to assassinate him. Under al-Ghalib the idea went into abeyance, and neither Abd al-Malik nor al-Mutawakkil had the time or, more likely, the inclination to revive it.

Ahmad al-Mansur, however, seems to have arrived with full-blown caliphal ambitions. Prophecies were dutifully produced, dreams recalled, and testimonies given that foretold his greatness. The Prophet himself was said to have predicted that Ahmad would be "the tinderbox from which the spark would burst forth." Al-Mansur's belief in himself must have been greatly re-inforced by the victory at Wadi al-Makhazin. Obviously his destiny would not be limited to the boundaries of Morocco. For inspiration he looked to the Caliphate of Cordoba, which had left a glorious legacy in art, architecture, and scholarship and had enjoyed considerable success in warfare against the Christian kingdoms of Iberia. Of the earlier states in Morocco, al-Mansur used as his model the Almohad Empire, which had claimed universal power and whose early leaders combined religious and political authority.

Caliphs were thought to be divinely chosen, yet they displayed certain outward signs that were obvious to the faithful. Al-Fishtali and others go to great lengths in emphasizing al-Mansur's moral qualities and his piety, two such signs. This sultan possessed all the character traits necessary for the position of caliph: Above all he was just; he was also compassionate, knowledgeable, generous, gentle, patient, successful in war, eager to seek counsel, and diligent in his religious duties. The image he projected was one of distinction and dignity. His physical attractiveness was another indicator of God's favor, at least according to al-Fishtali, who claimed that those who served God in high capacities were marked by a beautiful appearance. Mustafa al-Jannabi, who would have strongly opposed al-Mansur's claim to be caliph,

admitted that the new ruler of Marrakesh was "young and ro-
bust . . . sagacious and in awe of God. He has already attained a
degree of achievement more brilliant than any of his ancestors
and the kings nearest to him." In describing al-Mansur, al-Ifrani
notes that "his demeanor was affable, his manners gracious,
and his bearing elegant." In projecting an image of caliphal distinction and dignity, the Anonymous Chronicler of Fez struck
the only sour chords. He depicts al-Mansur as having a speech
impediment, wearing sumptuous clothing that dragged on the
ground, and being overweight with slender ankles so that "his
gait was not assured."

In claiming to be caliph, al-Mansur was announcing to the
world that he was no client of the Ottoman Empire and that
Morocco was not under Turkish influence. The lesson of history
was obvious: As the Battle of Lepanto had announced the passing
of Ottoman power, the Battle of Wadi al-Makhazin heralded the
rise of Sa'di power. Technically, since al-Mansur was caliph, the
Ottoman sultan owed him allegiance, and the Ottoman Empire,
like the rest of the Islamic world, including Persia and the
Mughal Empire of India, was an extension of the Empire of
Morocco. Al-Mansur had to be cautious about this: An ideological quarrel could not be allowed to spark another attempt
at assassination or invasion. In his direct correspondence with
Murad III, al-Mansur did not specifically assert that he was
caliph over all Muslims, although in a letter to Ottoman officials in Algiers, he once referred to Marrakesh as the "seat of
the caliphate."

If in fact any Muslim state of the day could have claimed
rights to the caliphate, it was the Ottoman Empire, and the sultan
in Constantinople often treated smaller Muslim polities as though
his empire constituted the caliphate. If the Ottoman sultan
rarely called himself Commander of the Faithful, he used other
titles associated with the role of caliph, the most important of
which was "Servant of the Two Holy Shrines," meaning the official protector of Mecca and Medina. For those who still held
the caliphate as an ideal, the Ottoman sultan was generally considered the ruling caliph.

The Ottomans did not pursue the caliphate concept as a central element in their ideology for very good reason: They did

not belong to the Quraysh tribe; they were not even Arabs. And if al-Mansur's claims could be dismissed as pretentious in light of the portion of Islam he actually controlled, he did have the right pedigree, which made his pretension a more serious matter. On al-Mansur's side, he does not seem to have considered the possibility that the caliphate could not be resurrected. Perhaps for the immediate future, he was thinking only in terms of a western caliphate; if so, this was a huge challenge that would necessitate driving the Turks out of North Africa. Al-Mansur certainly had such dreams. An interesting poem by a lesser court poet, al-Satibi, mentions al-Mansur's ultimate destiny but also refers to a more specific goal: "It is him that God has promised domination of the world and the conquest of the Pyramids." However, even if he succeeded in taking all of the African continent, he would be creating just another empire, not the universal caliphate, which by definition meant the union of all Muslims worldwide. Nor does al-Mansur seem to have taken into account the possibility that the majority of his co-religionists may have no longer wanted a caliphate—or that they might not have wanted him as their caliph. Perhaps he didn't care; the caliphate, after all, was not a democracy.

Propaganda and the Prophet's Birthday

As caliph, Ahmad al-Mansur assumed the title Imam of Islam. Imam ("one who stands in front") was most commonly used to refer to a prayer leader, but in a wider sense it could mean the leader of a Muslim community or, in the widest sense, leader of the worldwide community of Muslims. Titles were an important element in the well-orchestrated propaganda campaign that emanated from the Badi palace. Whenever al-Mansur's name was said, it was followed by his titles and words of praise. Prayers were chanted in his name. The Badi as a symbol of power and glory was itself part of this propaganda.

Along with the panegyrists, poets, apologists, and pamphleteers, al-Mansur employed chroniclers who were charged with writing official histories. The use of their talents was not limited to Morocco; in a largely illiterate age only important people read books, and this was the class the official chroniclers hoped to influence. Besides al-Fishtali, the most important of al-Mansur's court scholars was Ibn al-Qadi, a Fezi from a distinguished family who had studied in Egypt and had many contacts among the ulama of that country. Altogether he wrote at least forty treatises on subjects ranging from mathematics to law, of which ten have survived. His historical works, which have many digressions, attempt to be as much works of literature as of history; one of them is best described as a historical poem. In general, Ibn al-Qadi focuses more on the personal qualities of the ruler than on real historical issues, and his main theses were that Ahmad al-Mansur was the only ruler qualified to be caliph and that to obey the caliph was to obey God. Nevertheless, Ibn al-Qadi's work contains important factual material, and it was used by al-Ifrani.

Al-Mansur was anxious to employ Ibn al-Qadi because of his considerable reputation among ulama in lands to the east of Morocco and, in particular, because of his connections with scholars in Cairo. Ibn al-Qadi's task was to persuade such people to look favorably on al-Mansur's claim to the caliphate and to undermine Ottoman influence in the empire's greatest intellectual center. In his writings he contrasts how just the government was in Morocco with how unjust it was in Egypt. Ibn al-Qadi managed to win over several distinguished scholars, who exchanged letters with al-Mansur in which both sides congratulate and praise the other and al-Mansur's claim to be caliph is openly discussed and supported. What the caliph in Marrakesh could hope to get from his propaganda campaign in the east was, at most, an open call from those scholars to expand his rule over their lands, which were currently under the firm hand of the Ottomans. No such call ever came, and if it had, it is unlikely al-Mansur's armies could have answered it.

Ahmad al-Mansur had greater success in selling his image at home than abroad because his goal was clear and immediate: to stay in power and to provide legitimacy for his dynasty's rule. He proved to be a master of ritual and ceremonial display. The most successful example of this came in the celebration of the Prophet's birthday, the 'Id al-Mawlid, which was not originally part of the calendar of Islamic celebrations. In some places it began to be observed in the twelfth century, reaching the coast of Morocco in the late thirteenth, where it was promoted as an alternative to the popularity of Christmas. These early celebrations were highlighted by feasting, gift-giving, poetry reading, and the burning of candles. Al-Mansur made the Mawlid a national celebration, one of the three most important in Morocco, a sacred, collective ritual merging Islam with the Sa'di monarchy.

The central performance of the Mawlid took place in Marrakesh, with dignitaries from all over the country in attendance. On its eve, hundreds of huge white and red candles were mounted on litters and carried to the beat of drums in a procession past cheering crowds who thronged the streets. The candles were deposited at the main gate of the Badi palace for the night. Just before daybreak al-Mansur would appear in a white robe and lead the waiting crowd in prayer. The gate was then opened, allowing everyone to move into the courtyard. All the celebrants were men, and all were cloaked in long white robes with hoods covering much of their faces. Al-Mansur took his seat on the throne that had been positioned before the blazing candles. The crowd, organized into a hierarchy, marched in review according to rank, beginning with the qadis and ulama, then government officials, soldiers, and the general public. All were invited to participate in festivities that included poetry reading, story telling, plays, songs, dances, and the music of trumpets. The central themes of these performances were the life of the Prophet, his holiness, his bloodlines, and his descendants, especially al-Mansur. Those who gave the best performances were awarded prizes of gold and jewels. The event was concluded with a great feast in which all were invited to eat as much as they wanted.

When the dignitaries went home, they organized lesser versions of the ceremony that centered on lighted candles and recitations in praise of God, the Prophet, and the caliph. In this way the tie between God and the humblest of men living in the most remote corner of Morocco was renewed each year through the person of the caliph. Back in Marrakesh, the festivities continued for seven days as men carried around smaller candles on trays. On the seventh day the caliph led a procession to Muhammad al-Shaykh's tomb, and another round of poetry reading followed. The participants then returned to al-Badi, where al-Mansur distributed more gifts.

In the celebration of the Mawlid, love of God became identified with love of His Prophet, which in turn became identified with love of the Prophet's descendant, the caliph. The person of the caliph, surrounded by a great light, was the only one of the three actually present in a corporeal sense. The ruler came to represent all believers: He was the link to the divine. In this way, a ceremony whose purpose was to honor the Prophet Muhammad was turned into a celebration of the power, holiness, and sacredness—falling not far short of divinity—of the caliph, Ahmad al-Mansur.

Al-Fishtali reports that he wrote some poetry for inscription on the Badi walls and that al-Mansur vetoed it because it was too glowing and came too close to describing attributes belonging only to God. Al-Fishtali uses this incident as an example of al-Mansur's modesty, another caliphal trait. This story notwithstanding, al-Mansur came close to assuming qualities normally associated with divinity in another practice. He began to give audiences from behind a curtain, which gave the illusion of his being invisible or speaking with a heavenly voice. Once again, the caliph had separated himself from the rest of mankind and become rather more like the divine.

The Mahdi

Given the strict nature of Islamic monotheism, Ahmad al-Mansur had to be very careful: Divine figures in the Muslim world could quickly pass into the realm of heresy. The position of caliph was essentially a temporal one; al-Mansur needed a more sacred capacity that at the same time had a legitimate role within the fold of Islam. Poets and propagandists emphasized the lineal tie between the Prophet Muhammad and his descendant Ahmad al-Mansur as marking the beginning and end of an era. He would become the Mahdi, the "divinely guided one," sometimes roughly translated as "Messiah," an eschatological figure who would appear near the end of time, when the world was hopelessly corrupt. The clearest and most succinct explanation of the Mahdi comes from the fourteenth-century historian Ibn Khaldun:

> It has been (accepted) by all Muslims in every epoch, that at the end of time a man from the family (of the Prophet) will without

fail make his appearance, one who will strengthen Islam and make justice triumph. Muslims will follow him, and he will gain domination over the Muslim realm. He will be called the Mahdi. Following him, the Antichrist will appear, together with all the subsequent signs of the Day of Judgment. After the Mahdi, Jesus will descend and kill the Antichrist. Or, Jesus will descend together with the Mahdi, and help him kill the Antichrist.

Neither the Mahdi nor the Antichrist, referred to as al-Dajjal ("the Deceiver"), is mentioned in the Qur'an, but both appear in the *hadith* and other Islamic literature. The Mahdi arrives at a time of crisis and frustration to restore order, the strict observance of Islamic law, peace, and justice. Under him Islam will be carried to the entire world, but the Mahdi will die before the day of resurrection. The Qur'an stresses that resurrection will come at the end of time, when all will be judged and divided into the righteous, who will enjoy paradise, and the wicked, who will suffer damnation.

Ahmad al-Mansur was not Morocco's first Mahdi. The Almohad state had been founded by a Mahdi from the High Atlas, and the Sus Valley was a hotbed for Mahdist activity. One tradition, which existed before the rise of the Sa'dis and was known throughout Morocco, maintained that the Mahdi would appear as a *sharif* in the region of the Sus. This proclamation was supposedly attributed to the Prophet Muhammad. Al-Jazuli referred to himself as the Mahdi, claiming that his ancestor, the Prophet, had told him so in a dream, and he was recognized as such by his followers. Some sources refer to al-Qa'im as the Mahdi, although the title he took was meant for the herald of the Mahdi. His son, Muhammad al-Shaykh, took the title and is sometimes referred to in history books today as Muhammad al-Mahdi. He seemed satisfied merely to use the title as an honorific, and neither he nor anyone in his court pushed the theological arguments in support of such a claim. Al-Mansur had an inscription added to his father's tomb that referred to his father as the Mahdi. Presumably this was only propaganda, for by this time no world-ending event had taken place, a good indication that Muhammad al-Shaykh was no Mahdi.

It was a good time to assume the title of Mahdi in Morocco. The Islamic calendar, the Anno Hijra system of dating that began with Muhammad's flight to Medina, was approaching its millennium: the year A.H. 1000 would begin on October 19, 1591 C.E. Predictions of the arrival of the Mahdi and the end of the world had been made before, especially for the years A.H. 200 (815–816 C.E.) and A.H. 500 (1106–1107 C.E.). Trying to calculate exactly when the world would end had become a major intellectual exercise for certain scholars. According to one tradition, seven thousand years would separate the creation of the world from Judgment Day, with the Prophet Muhammad arriving after six thousand years. Extraordinary events, which Ibn Khaldun calls "signs," would signal a sequence of events that would culminate in the end of the world. The sun would rise in the west, and a series of calamities—famines, epidemics, natural catastrophes, wars, violent social upheavals—would befall mankind. In 1517 the final remnant of the Abbasid Caliphate disappeared, and the last nominal Abbasid caliph died in 1543, extinguishing the dynasty that had served for more than seven centuries. Many now looked to the coming of the Mahdi, who would inherit the earth and lead the faithful through the cataclysmic events that were approaching. With the apocalypse at hand, the forces of God had to be rallied, and who better to do that than a descendant of the Prophet, a *sharif* to whom all Muslims would swear allegiance.

Ahmad al-Mansur did not claim outright that he was the Mahdi, nor did his officials, secretaries, or chroniclers refer to him as "Mahdi." At most, some court-generated poetry insinuated it (one poem said that al-Mansur will "receive the vanguard of Jesus Christ"). Rather, his claim to be Mahdi was delivered in a subtle manner through the use of symbol and metaphor. The supernatural elements integral to his life—the visions, predictions, and prophecies—were all signs of his special nature. He began his reign with a great victory in jihad, and many Muslims believed that the Mahdi's conquest of the world would begin with the defeat of the Iberian Christians, followed by the reconquest of Andalusia. His character, his deeds, and the way he lived his life, as reported by his propaganda machine, matched common assumptions about the Mahdi. As this became evident, people would draw their own conclusions. Many were, after all, looking for the Mahdi.

Al-Mansur's coyness in openly declaring himself the Mahdi should not be a surprise. There should be only one caliph at a time, but there would be only one Mahdi for all time. Declaring oneself the Mahdi carried with it an extraordinary accountability. If indeed the millennium did not mark the beginning of the end of the world, al-Mansur might still salvage his credibility—unlike all earlier self-professed Mahdis.

The Sincerity Issue

Al-Mansur's waffling over the Mahdi issue did not spare him from the critics. They saw his claims and his insinuations as being extraordinarily pretentious for a man whose sharifian ancestry was suspect, at least among Morocco's more established *shurafa* families, and whose dynasty had been in power for little more than half a century. They regarded his use of grandiloquent titles as little more than a rationale for behaving arrogantly, which in their eyes he seemed to do whenever it suited him. Western writers, both contemporary observers and later historians, like to see al-Mansur as the Islamic version of Machiavelli's prince, manipulating even religion, by far the most potent force in his world, solely for the purposes of personal power and wealth. To António de Saldanha, he was the "grand master of hypocrisy," but to al-Fishtali he was "the caliph of the caliphs," and a poem etched on the Badi walls says that he "strikes fear, even to the far side of Iraq," which was more wish than reality. Certainly one of his greatest goals was the establishment of a western caliphate, which in time would be expanded first to include all Arabs and ultimately all Muslims.

Yet al-Mansur's strivings and ambitions must be seen as more than a simple lust for power. The skepticism that permeates modern Western historiography too easily disentangles religion from politics, wealth, and the longings of ego. Ahmad al-Mansur may not have been quite so cynical. He was a man who remained conscious of his own destiny even if deliberate self-promotion was an integral part of fulfilling that destiny. The image of al-Mansur's plotting in his own mind how he would use religious symbols and images to exploit the gullibility of his people with the implication that he knew, deep down, that it was all a lot of mumbo-jumbo, is a twenty-first-century image imposed on a time and place where it is ill-fitting. It's too simple. If his behavior in dealing with foreigners and countrymen alike belied his own ideology, this was probably less a matter of conscious fraud than the result of his own confusion. He was a man caught between different worlds.

Land of Gold

Figure 5.1 North and West Africa, Late Sixteenth Century. Courtesy of author.

Power comes at a price, and finances remained the most pressing problem throughout al-Mansur's reign. In the best of times, the Moroccan tax collection system was inefficient. Much of the burden lay on the peasantry, whose agricultural production was limited by outdated technology. A large part of the tax revenue was kept by those who collected it, with only a portion reaching the royal coffers. Whole chunks of the Moroccan populace completely escaped the unpleasantness of being taxed, foremost of whom were desert and mountain tribesmen, who simply evaded payment, and the religious establishment, whose members claimed exemption under Islamic law. The merchants of the urban centers, smug behind their city walls, were reluctant to contribute their portion, convinced they were not getting their money's worth from the central government. As António de Saldanha put it, "no one pays [taxes] unless forced to do so." The general attitude was that the Sa'dis could be the nation's religious leaders and even claim political power, but to levy taxes for general expenses was beyond their purview.

Income and Expenditures

Much of the task of turning Moroccans into taxpayers had fallen on Muhammad al-Shaykh. He instituted new exactions, most of which specialists in Islamic law declared illegal. Nevertheless, he enforced their collection with uncustomary vigor, bringing on a chronic tax rebellion, particularly among the tribes of the Atlas Mountains. Putting down the uprisings placed an additional burden on the treasury. When al-Shaykh was assassinated, he was leading an expedition against just such a tax rebellion.

Raising new taxes was not the only strategy of the Sa'dis for stabilizing government finances. Expanding trade and commerce and encouraging the production of cash crops for export were tried, with some success. The principal crop became sugar, for which Morocco had been reputed since the twelfth century, when al-Idrisi, the most influential geographer of his day, noted: "In the Sus they make a sugar that is known throughout the world . . . it surpasses all others in taste and purity." Al-Shaykh revived the industry and extended governmental control over it. For a time thereafter, it is estimated that one-third of the state's income came from the profits of the sugar industry.

The Moroccans had a ready customer in the English, who seemed to have a limitless appetite for sugar. By the mid 1570s England was importing more than 600,000 pounds of refined sugar annually from Morocco, plus unrefined sugar and sugar products like hard candy and marmalade. For the most part, the Moroccans bartered their sugar for artillery, handguns, ammunition, gunpowder, and materials for use in their own weapons industry. Morocco, it seemed, was a bottomless pit for ordnance.

When al-Mansur came to the throne, the economy was booming—at least according to al-Fishtali, who maintains that the management of foreign trade and control over sugar and other industries (especially mining and munitions manufacturing) allowed the government to be mild in its exactions on its subjects. This version of events is not supported by European observers, who were of one voice in commenting on the heavy burden carried by the Moroccan taxpayer. A Spaniard, Diego de Torres, summed it up: "In a word, this Tyrant is the absolute master of everything his subjects own." Nor was international trade the answer to Morocco's financial woes, despite the congratulations of al-Fishtali. English weapons for Moroccan sugar were an example of swapping overvalued manufactured products for undervalued raw material. And there was a limit to what sugar and such Moroccan products as dates, almonds, and gum arabic could buy. Even if the Moroccans were selling their products for cash, foreign trade with Europe could not provide profit enough to support a government involved in chronic warfare, much of which was aimed at collecting its own taxes.

Although Sa'di financial problems did not begin under Ahmad al-Mansur, they grew worse. A more centralized government was a more expensive government, and a professional army that was not plundering its enemies or being rented out to fight someone else's wars constituted a permanent drain on the treasury. The maintenance of an ostentatious court and the continuing arms buildup cost even more than the self-proclaimed Caliph of All the Muslims had. Building the Badi palace brought the treasury to a fiscal precipice. Such problems, however, were not evident to the casual observer. This was a state that appeared to be rich: "The Kingdoms of Barbarie [Fez and Marrakesh] reached the highest degree of grandeur they had ever attained," gushed António de Saldanha in describing conditions in the late 1580s. Peace and security allowed for a great expansion in trade and commence "from which the sharif [al-Mansur] has made very large profits." Al-Mansur cultivated the image of an opulent potentate, pursuing a policy of grandeur Europeans would later associate with the romance of Ali Baba and the *Thousand and One Nights*. Yet this potentate spent his entire reign trying to find sources of income to match his expenditures.

Not that al-Mansur let the state's financial woes cramp his style. Despite the chronic need for cash, he was extravagantly generous in a very public way to anyone who pleased him, from flattering courtiers and compliant ulama to European work-men. He gave money to the poor and the needy and to impor-tant men who visited him. He used it to free captives (including some Jews) held for ransom by Christian corsairs, and he paid for the circumcision ceremonies of poor boys. He gave away so much money, according to his court writers, it was impossible to count it. One of their poems compared him to a cloud full of water—except that al-Mansur would burst with gold and silver rather than rain. Al-Fishtali claimed that he gave away over a thousand silver coins when the mood struck him, and al-Ifrani notes that "he had a nature so lavish that he gave without counting and distributed his money in gifts, as a man who did not fear poverty." Such largess in the face of looming deficits is another disconnect in the complexities of al-Mansur. The only suitable explanation is that generosity was considered an im-portant characteristic of the Mahdi. In one *hadith* the Prophet was reputed to have said: "At the end of my community there will be a caliph who will pour out money without reckoning." If al-Mansur was determined to be recognized as the Mahdi, he needed to pay the price.

Al-Mansur did not begin his reign with money problems. Safely in his clutches was the ransom for a large part of one na-tion's nobility. For a while so much money from Portugal poured into Morocco that Ahmad al-Mansur may have acquired the additional title of al-Dhahabi, "the Golden," although that title may not have been assumed until 1591. The enormous windfall may have given al-Mansur an unrealistic feeling of fi-nancial security. The flow of ransom money would eventually dry up, but al-Mansur's taste for what it could buy would not.

Except in highly unusual circumstances, governments are ex-pected to depend on taxes for most of their funding, and here al-Mansur suffered the same problems his father had. When the tribesmen of the mountains and the desert who had rallied to the Sa'di dynasty at Wadi al-Makhazin returned home, once again they refused to pay taxes. On his part, al-Mansur did not hesitate to impose what al-Ifrani calls "considerable sums and extraordinary contributions," adding "heavy burdens" to what his father had inflicted. This led to widespread misery and deep resentment. When the people "complained," according to al-Ifrani, al-Mansur showed that he "was not stingy with the blood of his subjects and did not hesitate to let it flow on occasion."

Despite frequent statements emphasizing that his number one priority as ruler was to enforce Islamic law, al-Mansur's taxes, like those of his father, fell largely beyond the bounds of what the Qur'an sanctioned. Al-Mansur justified this by pointing out that the Land of Islam was threatened—a reference to the ever-convenient Spanish and Portuguese—and as ruler of Morocco he was charged with maintaining order, which could be accomplished only with a strong army paid for by taxes. These were exceptional times, and as Imam and Commander of the Faithful, he was above the rules that governed men in normal times. He was the leader of the worldwide jihad, and he was responsible for preparing the community to meet the millennium. With the struggle between good and evil on the line, he could hardly be bothered about technicalities concerning who and what could and could not be taxed. And on top of taxes, he made people pay rent on the pretext that the land belonged to him by right of conquest, invoking the Islamic invasion of North Africa in the seventh century; as a descendant of the Prophet, he was thus the rightful claimant to all land.

The tax revolt did not completely disappear during al-Mansur's reign, but he did not suffer the chronic conditions approaching civil war that his father had faced. This was not because al-Mansur's arguments were more convincing. Rather, under him the central government was more powerful, and all but the most implacable of tax protesters became reluctant to challenge the government's large and well-equipped force of professionals.

Under al-Mansur the state attempted to exert as much control over the economy as possible, which meant operating monopolies in some of the more lucrative industries and leasing out others. The Sa'dis had been doing this with sugar production for decades, but the English had recently found another Moroccan product they needed. Saltpeter (potassium nitrate) was a necessary ingredient in gunpowder, and no natural deposits were available in England. Morocco had tons of it. But this was a sticky matter because the Moroccan ulama considered unlawful the sale of any material that might strengthen the enemies of Islam, and the English were, after all, Christians. Consequently, al-Mansur officially banned the sale of Moroccan saltpeter to all Christians. However, this did not mean he had to obey his own law if the return were high enough. At first, his agents insisted they would take only cannonballs as payment for saltpeter, but the demand became too great, and in 1581 Queen Elizabeth authorized the trade of naval timber as well. Four years later her government granted a charter to a group of merchants to form the Barbary Company to control all English trade with Morocco. The first agent of this company also served as the queen's ambassador in Marrakesh.

The English did not find al-Mansur the ideal trading partner they had hoped. He was, they complained, the kind of businessman who demanded quick payment and good service but who could be dilatory and deceptive when it came to fulfilling his part of a bargain. In commercial matters, as in diplomatic and military matters, his deeds often did not match his words. Ultimately the Barbary Company did not turn out to be a successful venture, for which al-Mansur's shortsighted business practices were blamed in part, and the English went elsewhere. As for his own people, apparently he felt he could not trust them in important commercial matters. The sultan farmed out state monopolies to Jews, often of Spanish origin, and to some European merchants who became very rich as a result. The state benefited, although government interference in the economy did not guarantee a rich state, only a state in which the government could make decisions that benefited itself and not necessarily the populace at large.

If taxes did not cover the basic costs of government administration and defense—leaving aside the frivolities to which al-Mansur treated himself—neither would sugar and saltpeter. When the money from Wadi al-Makhazin ran out, al-Mansur's gaze fixed on a new direction, his final hope for financial security. The Moroccans had a saying: "As tar cures the gall of a camel, so poverty finds its unfailing remedy in the Sudan." Morocco was an important terminus for the trans-Saharan gold trade that came up from the Western Sudan, a large savanna region that extended laterally across the interior of West Africa. The obvious way to alleviate a spate of economic and political problems was to obtain a much larger infusion of gold than peaceful commerce could bring. However, a Moroccan army large enough to conquer the interior of West Africa, it was commonly believed, could not survive a desert crossing, and a force small enough to make the crossing would be overwhelmed in battle. Besides, in their commercial relations with the African interior, the Moroccans had little to complain about. Mostly they traded finished goods for raw materials and served as middlemen for European products, another overvalued-for-undervalued swap, this time to the benefit of Morocco.

Nevertheless, to make Morocco rich and powerful and to ensure the future of the dynasty, the Sa'dis began to think about seizing control of the trans-Saharan trade, in particular the commerce in gold. They never developed a blueprint or even a plan of execution for this, and they certainly did not set out to conquer the Sahara, much less the lands beyond it. But Morocco had had long-term interests in the Sahara and the West African interior even if the specific policies addressing those interests varied widely according to who was in power.

The Trans-Saharan Trade

As southerners with their roots in the Dar'a and Sus valleys, the Sa'dis had seen caravans bringing gold and other riches from across the desert for centuries. Watching the camels come and go, they probably developed an inflated idea of the wealth this trade represented. Gaining control over the gold trade, however, was a challenge. Perhaps this could be accomplished by occupying its termini, the cities on the northern side of the desert. Perhaps the Sa'dis would have to push into the desert itself, occupying the oases through which the trade flowed as well as the salt mines, for salt was the major item of barter for gold. Perhaps in the end the Moroccans would have to cross the desert and capture the source of the gold, although given the risk, that would be a last-case scenario.

The trans-Saharan trade carried a variety of products from across North Africa, Europe, and western Asia, for which the

West Africans paid with their own specialties. West African goods ranged from the very exotic, like civet (a musky secretion used in making perfumes that came from a gland near the sexual organ of the male civet cat, a species of African wildcat) and "grains of paradise" (an African variety of pepper), to the not-so-exotic, like slaves. But the glitter in this trade came from gold. North Africans, Arabs, and Europeans were all aware that sometime during the Middle Ages, West Africa had become the major source of the gold used in their coinage. Exactly where in West Africa the gold came from was the closely guarded secret of a class of Sudanese merchants known as the Wangara. To the outside world, Wangara was thought to be a place rather than a people, a mythical land of gold. In fact, the gold came from various sources around West Africa that were prominent at different times. By Ahmad al-Mansur's day, the major producer of gold was the Akan goldfields region located north of the Portuguese fort at Mina.

Although statistics are nonexistent, the best guess is that the trans-Saharan gold trade peaked in the late fourteenth century, and West African gold made possible the great increase in international trade during the Late Middle Ages. The Great Bullion Famine of the fifteenth century in Europe was followed in the sixteenth century by the Great Price Revolution, a time of steadily increasing inflation. From about the middle of that century, the huge influx of silver and gold from the New World started to kick in, but the price revolution had begun even before American metals made their impact. In the days before paper money, European governments frantically sought to expand the supply of precious metals to keep up with the rise in prices, which meant reopening old mines and exerting additional pressure on outside sources like West Africa to increase production.

A commerce like the gold trade needed protection, which on the southern end was provided in sequence by three great empires. The first was the Kingdom of Ghana, a going concern by the eighth century and perhaps much earlier. Ghana's decline in the twelfth century led to the rise of Mali, which was larger, stronger, and richer than its predecessor. As Mali began to contract in the fifteenth century, the third and largest of these empires, Songhay, appeared as the dominant power. When Ahmad al-Mansur looked to the south, beyond the Tuareg tribesmen of the Sahara to the land where the gold came from, he saw Songhay and its two great cities, the ancient capital of Gao on the eastern bend of the Niger River and the commercial center of Timbuktu on the western edge of the bend.

Photo 5.2   The market at Timbuktu looks much as it did when the city was at the center of the gold trade. Courtesy of author.

The Songhay Empire

In al-Mansur's day, Songhay was an ancient kingdom. Its fifteenth king is reported to have converted to Islam in the tenth century, but that did not signal a rapid Islamization of the rest of society. It didn't even initiate a religious trickledown beyond the court and the army. Nor did the king himself completely disavow the traditional practices of the old religion when they reinforced his own position. As for the peasants and fishermen who were the vast majority of his subjects, their lives revolved around daily interaction with the spirit world. Most of them had absolutely no interest in an omnipotent universal deity that somehow dwelled outside nature and whose secrets were kept in writings they couldn't read and whose stories were about people who lived in unknown lands.

During the sixteenth century Songhay was under the Askiya dynasty, Askiya becoming also a title signifying "Emperor." Working from their base in the Middle Niger Valley, Songhay armies spilled across the grasslands of the Western Sudan, north into the Sahara and south to the borderlands of the tropical forest. Songhay became the largest African state of its time and, for a while, one of the world's most impressive empires.

The first Askiya, Muhammad Turé, took Islam more seriously than most of his predecessors or successors. Once his throne was secure, he made a two-year pilgrimage to the Holy Cities, from which he returned with an official appointment from the Abbasid caliph in Cairo to serve as *khalifa*, which in this sense meant deputy for the Western Sudan, not caliph over all Islam. But even Askiya Muhammad made no attempt at a forcible mass conversion, which would have ripped his empire apart. He is generally considered to have been the best ruler of his dynasty, but he quite literally sowed the seeds that would help to bring his great state low. Exactly how many children he sired is unknown, but the largest count, from a marginal note in a chronicle by the Timbuktu scholar Mahmud Kati, claims 471! The other great chronicle of Timbuktu, by Abd al-Rahman al-Sadi, observes only that the Askiya had so many children he ran out of names, leaving some to share another's name.

The most important positions in the Songhay government were held by the royal family. Brothers and cousins became both the foundation of central power and at the same time the major threat to it. The first act of a new Askiya was to determine which of his relatives he could trust. The loyal ones would be rewarded with high posts, and those who posed a threat would be eliminated. Survivors rarely felt beholden. Nor did they adhere to a sense of fair play or practice patience in awaiting their turns to take the reigns of power. The dynastic history of Songhay is characterized by civil wars, coups, regicide, and fratricide in which the sons, nephews, and grandsons of Askiya Muhammad killed each other with gusto. Although murder was common, and the state prison often bulged with members of the royal family, the pool of potential plotters was so large it was never exhausted.

Chronic succession crises gradually sapped the power of the Songhay Empire, which had deep ethnic, religious, and geographical divisions. Yet the empire creaked along until the last decade of the sixteenth century, secure only because of a lack of foreign adversaries. Of the eight Askiyas who succeeded Muhammad Turé between 1529 and 1591, one, Dawud, ruled for thirty-three years (1549–1582); the other seven together ruled for just thirty years. Dawud was the most capable of them, but he also enjoyed one great advantage: By the time he ascended the throne, a sizeable number of his brothers and cousins were dead, having largely killed each other off.

After Askiya Dawud, the rivalry for the throne shifted from his brothers to his sons. The next nine years would see three brothers succeed each other and a fourth lead a revolt that almost toppled the whole edifice. This upheaval, which began in 1588, was led by Muhammad al-Sadiq, the Balama, or commander of imperial troops in the western half of the empire. It became a civil war of west versus east, Timbuktu versus Gao, the more Muslim side of the empire versus the more traditional side. The east won. The Balama was killed, and a reign of terror was directed at all officials who were thought to have been his accomplices. A great number were executed, often cudgeled to death or buried alive. The provinces of the west that had provided many of the soldiers in the rebel army were ravaged. The retaliation may have proved gratifying to those in Gao, but it was self-defeating for the empire as a whole. The civil war had already weakened the empire, and thousands of soldiers had been killed. In the aftermath virtually all experienced government personnel in the west were purged. From the outside, the Songhay Empire appeared strong economically and weak politically, a plum ripe for the plucking. Across the Sahara lay Morocco and Ahmad al-Mansur, a sultan in search of a panacea.

Into the Sahara

During the early sixteenth century, while the Moroccans were busy fighting the Portuguese and each other, Songhay power reached far into the Sahara. Many nomadic tribesmen, foremost of whom were the veil-wearing, camel-rearing Tuaregs, accepted the suzerainty of the Askiya and became clients of the Songhay Empire. Gao depended on them to police the Sahara and to act as a first line of defense against intrusions that might come from the north. By controlling the Tuaregs, Songhay dominated the power axis that ran from the Niger River to the oasis of Tuwat and the salt deposits at Taghaza, the largest and most important mine in the central Sahara. Lying between Morocco to the northwest, Tunis to the northeast, and Timbuktu and Gao to the south, Tuwat was the gateway to North Africa from the south. Tuwat does not seem to have been officially part of the Songhay Empire, but the ruling merchant oligarchy was friendly and accommodating in its dealings with Gao, and it had no love for the Moroccan sultan.

In 1526 a Sa'dian force had occupied Tuwat, then withdrawn to deal with more pressing matters, including the wars with the Wattasids and Turks and the subsequent tax revolts. When Sa'di interest returned to the Sahara, it fixed on the Taghaza salt mine, which lay almost equidistant (570 miles) between Marrakesh and Timbuktu. For centuries the mine had been subject to tribal confederations, until the Songhay officially assumed control under Askiya Muhammad. Taghaza had never been incorporated into a Moroccan state, but the Sa'dis began to claim it as part of their domains. Not that Morocco needed the salt; the white slabs that came out of the mine would continue to be sent south, as had been done for centuries. By controlling Saharan salt, however, the Moroccans hoped to control West African gold. The importance of salt to the peoples of West Africa—a hot land where perspiration leeched the human body—can scarcely be exaggerated. For centuries its major source had been Saharan rock salt formed when ancient inland seas dried up. This salt was so dense it could be cut into blocks, put on the backs of camels, and carried over long distances.

The Sa'dis were not too shy to ask for something when they wanted it. In a letter delivered by an emissary, probably in 1540 or 1541, Ahmad al-A'raj "invited" the Songhay Askiya, Ishaq I, to give up Taghaza. The Moroccans, the sultan argued, were engaged in a holy war against the Christians that required the support of fellow Muslims, and Songhay could best help the cause by handing over its rich mine. Ishaq is reported by al-Sadi to have replied: "The Ahmad who will offer such counsel is not yet the emperor of Morocco and the Ishaq who will hear it is not me; this Ishaq has yet to be born." As a demonstration of the Askiya's power, Ishaq sent a force of two thousand Tuaregs to ravage the Dar'a Valley. The Taghaza issue was deferred, not settled, in Songhay's favor—for the time being.

Under Muhammad al-Shaykh, Moroccan attention focused first on a different part of the Sahara. He dispatched 1,800 cavalry across Mauritania in 1543–1544, probably with the intention of reopening the almost defunct western branch of the trans-Saharan trade route. The expedition reached the city of Wadan before turning back on receiving intelligence that the "King of Timbuktu" had sent a force of 300,000 to intercept it. In fact no such force ever existed, and the officer in charge may have made up this "intelligence" as an excuse to return home. In 1556–1557 an opportunity developed in Taghaza. Using as a pretext a squabble between two men of the same family, both of whom wanted the job of governor of Taghaza, who was a Gao appointee, al-Shaykh sent a force that surprised some Tuareg merchants in the process of loading salt and killed several of them. Askiya Dawud responded by authorizing salt merchants to open another deposit at a recently discovered site. Left with no merchants to take the salt, the Moroccans withdrew. Muhammad al-Shaykh was assassinated shortly after the attack on Taghaza, and under the less aggressive al-Ghalib tensions between Morocco and Songhay eased. The Songhay returned and reopened the mine at Taghaza.

Shortly after the Battle of Wadi al-Makhazin, al-Mansur sent a message to Askiya Dawud requesting that the Songhay give up a year of tax income from the Taghaza mines to support the Muslim jihad. Dawud responded with a gift of ten thousand mithqals (a mithqal weighed about 4.25 grams) of gold. Thereafter the two states enjoyed a period of détente that lasted through al-Mansur's first and Dawud's last years on their respective thrones. Although they never met, each professed to have had a close personal relationship with the other. When Dawud died, al-Mansur proclaimed a period of mourning during which high officials came to offer their condolences for the loss of his friend.

On the accession of Dawud's successor, Askiya al-Hajj, al-Mansur sent an embassy loaded with gifts as a profession of friendship. The real objective of this mission, however, was to gather information on the political and military situation in the Songhay Empire and to establish a network of spies and agents. The Askiya sent back presents worth twice what he had received, among them civet cats and eighty eunuchs. Al-Mansur then requested a subsidy, which al-Hajj granted. Al-Sadi, who reports on these doings, gives no indication whether al-Hajj knew of al-Mansur's subterfuge. In either case, the Askiya's generosity again left the sultan without a grievance. The Songhay would not, however, indulge al-Mansur in his desire to be recognized as caliph.

Shortly after he had assumed the title of caliph, al-Mansur sent messages to the Islamic rulers of sub-Saharan Africa demanding their allegiance. The response was mostly negative, although at least two showed some interest. The more important one was Mai Idris Aloma, the King of Bornu in the Lake Chad region. He was having trouble with the Turks, and although two thousand miles of desert separated Morocco from Bornu, he must have been thinking of the old adage about my enemy's enemies being my friends. The relationship between Bornu and the Ottoman Empire had once been cordial, and the Turks had provided Bornu with firearms and horses for its wars against non-Muslim neighbors. In 1577, however, the Ottomans invaded the Fezzan, a large oasis region in southern Libya whose rulers had traditionally paid allegiance to Bornu. At some time the Turks appear to have invaded Bornu itself from Egypt, but the desert crossing so debilitated the survivors that they were soundly defeated.

By 1582–1583 Mai Idris was sufficiently alarmed to turn to al-Mansur. He sent an embassy to Morocco that met with al-Mansur to request firearms and a corps of musketeers. The Bornu ambassador was informed that he could have them, but Mai Idris would have to take the bay'a, the oath of allegiance, to al-Mansur. The ambassador agreed, and al-Fishtali prepared a written document to be taken back and signed. It stated that God had confided the protection of Islam to al-Mansur, Commander of the Faithful and God's Vicar on Earth, and any Muslim who did not recognize his authority was a heretic—meaning, in effect, that disobedience to the caliph was disobedience to God.

Reports are conflicting as to whether the document was ever signed by both parties, and no record exists of firearms or a corps of musketeers going from Morocco to Bornu. Had the document been signed, al-Mansur would have been deluding himself if he thought that he would exercise authority over Bornu; Mai Idris Aloma, a great king in his own right, had no intention of taking orders from Marrakesh. On a practical level, the arrangement has been interpreted as an alliance against the Ottoman Empire, although if war had come on one front or the other, the logistical problems in one side's providing aid to the other would have been insurmountable.

In the same year as the Bornu agreement, al-Mansur moved to take care of outstanding matters involving Tuwat. The Turks in Algiers were showing interest in the oasis, and in 1579 they had made a less-than-determined attempt to take it. On his part, Al-Mansur was misinformed by advisers who led him to believe that Tuwat was richer than it was. In 1581 he sent an expedition toward Tuwat, but it was ambushed and its leader killed. Two years later the Sa'di army returned in force. Along the way it made a point of intimidating potentially rebellious tribes, devastating the countryside and executing members of recalcitrant families. Once the army reached Tuwat, "diverse summons were made repeatedly to the inhabitants to make an act of submission," al-Ifrani reports, "but possessed by the demon, they refused to do so; they were attacked thus and after a battle so fierce that it lasted several days, God subdued these rebels." The lesson worked for a while, and soon representatives from the central government were busy collecting taxes from sedentary and nomadic tribes alike. But al-Mansur's government demanded a lot of money, too much from tribesmen who were used to paying nothing. Within five years of the conquest, al-Mansur had to deal with three major uprisings, including one led by the local leaders he had appointed to represent his interests.

By taking Tuwat, al-Mansur controlled the northern half of the central trans-Saharan route. In 1584 his interests turned to the west. An army of twenty thousand, according to al-Sadi, was dispatched with orders to cross the desert through Wadan, then "head for the river," seizing all towns along the way until it reached Timbuktu. Which river is unclear; the Moroccans did not distinguish the Senegal from the Niger. If they wanted to reach Timbuktu and attack the Songhay Empire, they would have to get to the Niger, but their route took them more in the direction of the Senegal. If their real motive was to conquer Mauritania and rejuvenate the western branch of the trans-Saharan route, the enterprise was ill-conceived. Not much trade came by this route because the people at the other end had few products to send north other than slaves. António de Saldanha maintains that the immediate objective was the Kingdom of Janqueta (Chinguetti, a town near Wadan), but the ultimate destination was the Songhay Empire. The Moroccans were trying to find a way of getting there that would avoid the central trans-Saharan crossing, which traversed some of the worst sand seas in the desert. Taken together, al-Mansur's Tuwat and Mauritanian policies could have had only one goal: to control both termini of the trans-Saharan trade on his side of North Africa. For the western route, however, this seemed hardly worth the effort.

Al-Fishtali reports that the Moroccans took ninety days to cross Mauritania, finally arriving at a great river. There they terrorized the local tribes, gained their submission to the caliph, and levied some taxes before turning back. A much less favorable account is found in the Anonymous Chronicler of Fez, who maintains that al-Mansur decided to punish some of his troops "who refused obedience to him for a reason that we will leave in silence." He sent them into the Mauritanian Sahara, "then their guide, following the orders he had received from the sultan, fled so that losing their way in the desert they perished." One man alone returned to tell the tale. Al-Sadi's account tends to support this, although it is vague and less dramatic, noting only that "God decimated this army, which stricken with misfortune from hunger and thirst, dispersed in all directions. The survivors returned to their country without having accomplished their mission."

The most detailed account of the Mauritanian expedition is from António de Saldanha, who notes that the sultan was having difficulty paying his soldiers and hoped to diminish their numbers by sending a sizeable force—5,000 soldiers and 3,000 support personnel and merchants—on a dangerous mission. The expedition reached Chinguetti, but the local people tricked the qa'id in charge, then burned their own houses and fled. This qa'id proved to be extremely incompetent, and eventually the expedition ran out of food. The qa'id gave the order "every man for himself," then abandoned his army and left on horseback. Only he, his son, and one Christian slave made it back to Morocco. Al-Mansur made the best of a bad situation by confiscating the qa'id's property, which he used to defray the cost of the expedition. He also rid himself of some soldiers who, António de Saldanha believed, were potential mutineers.

Al-Mansur was not to be dissuaded by a disaster or two. The failure of his western enterprise was followed a year later by yet another grab for Taghaza: Two hundred musketeers were sent to seize the mine. No resistance was offered; forewarned, the inhabitants abandoned the place. Henceforth the Askiya forbade any merchant who was doing business in the Songhay Empire from dealing in Taghaza salt. The traders moved to a new mine at Taoudeni, which lay almost ninety miles closer to Timbuktu than Taghaza. With no traders arriving in Taghaza, the musketeers returned to Marrakesh.

Foiled again, Ahmad al-Mansur was at his wit's end. From his intelligence-gathering network, he knew the Songhay Empire had reached its nadir in a series of mostly self-inflicted misfortunes. If the Moroccans hesitated, a more vigorous ruler might come along to lead the Songhay out of the doldrums. Or a new imperial state might arise in the Western Sudan to replace the Songhay Empire, much as it had replaced Mali. Worse, the Turks might decide to strike from their bases in the northern Sahara and overrun the Songhay Empire, cutting off Morocco to the south. Al-Mansur saw a window of opportunity that might soon be closed.

Al-Mansur was receiving information from trans-Saharan merchants, but this had become insufficient for making the decision that had now become imminent. He sent two scholars who were noted Qur'anic specialists as a courtesy to the Askiya's court, escorted by two Andalusians and two renegades. All were spies. After gathering considerable intelligence, particularly on the gold trade, they returned to Marrakesh with a bonus: a letter from a nephew of the Askiya promising obedience and pledging his services should the caliph decide to send an army to Gao.

Matters of finance were pressing. The ransom money from the Portuguese was long gone, and the gifts from Dawud and al-Hajj had been spent. In 1589 the Moroccan dinar had to be devalued. Recent military operations—the taking of Tuwat, the second Mauritanian expedition, and the second Taghaza occupation—had cost a lot and brought little return. The Taghaza fiasco had cast doubt on the long-held Sa'dian maxim that Saharan salt was the key to Sudanese gold. Occupying Taghaza was not the solution; the only alternative was to go straight for the gold.

A CLOSER LOOK

Sources from Outside Morocco

Ahmad al-Mansur's impact beyond Morocco can be seen in the writings of contemporary and near-contemporary observers who lived as far afield as Timbuktu in one direction and Cambridge, England, in another. These sources range from mildly sympathetic to highly critical in their attitudes toward al-Mansur, but taken together they provide a more detached perspective than do the internal Moroccan sources.

Once al-Mansur had become involved in the affairs of the West African interior, he came to the attention of two chroniclers from Timbuktu. The history of the Songhay Empire is known today largely because of the survival of the *Tarikh al-Sudan*, by Abd al-Rahman al-Sadi, and the *Tarikh al-Fattash*, attributed to Mahmud Kati. Without them, the Western Sudan from the fourteenth to the seventeenth centuries would be largely a civilization lost to memory. Both authors came from the Timbuktu ulama. Al-Sadi, who lived in the first half of the seventeenth century, was employed as imam in several mosques and as a high-level secretary and occasional diplomat for the government. At some time during the period of his public service, al-Sadi decided to write a great history "because learning is rich in beauty and fertile in its teaching." The *Tarikh al-Sudan*, or Chronicle of the Land of the Black People, recounts happenings from the perspective of "the Muslims," meaning largely al-Sadi's own class, which by his time bore a significant grudge against al-Mansur. Nevertheless, in most instances al-Sadi plays the role of good chronicler, registering the facts as he saw or heard about them.

The *Tarikh al-Sudan* also provides interpretation, making it more than just a chronicle. It is moralistic, and its points are not presented subtly: It is the story of man being bad and God punishing him. Moral lapses led to social disorder, which in turn produced misfortunes that included both man-made and natural disasters.

The *Tarikh al-Sudan's* companion work, the *Tarikh al-Fattash,* or Chronicle of the Seeker, focuses on the golden age of the Songhay Empire under the Askiyas. If the *Tarikh al-Sudan* is the best, the *Tarikh al-Fattash* is the earliest surviving history written by a West African. Its authorship, however, remains a point of debate. The work is said to have been started by Mahmud Kati in 1519, and its last recorded event takes place in 1664. Its completion is attributed to Mahmud Kati's grandson, Ibn al-Mukhtar, but there is a problem about its dating even if one accepts the claim that Mahmud Kati lived to the age of 125. The *Tarikh al-Fattash* also includes mythical material—miracles, jinns, and other fantasies—mixed with history. This need not detract from its usefulness in supplementing the *Tarikh al-Sudan,* although if modern historians had to rely solely and literally on the *Tarikh al-Fattash,* they would conclude that the Western Sudan was a strange place indeed.

A description of both the Western Sudan and Morocco in the period during which the Sa'dis rose to power, the early years of the sixteenth century, is provided in the well-known account of Leo Africanus (al-Hasan b. Muhammad al-Wazzani). Leo, a Moroccan traveler, was captured by Christian pirates and ended up working for the Pope, writing about places he was said to have visited. An English translation of his chronicle appeared in 1600, the work of John Pory, a young scholar out of Cambridge University with an interest in cosmography. Pory felt sufficiently confident to add both a long preface that begins with a general commentary on Africa and an appendix on "The Great Princes of Africa." In the latter, Pory refers to al-Mansur as the "Xeriffo," or "Zeriffo," and gives useful information about the sultan's finances and military. This material is second-hand, for Pory himself did not visit Morocco but drew on information from English merchants who did.

The accounts of three other contemporaries came from men representing governments that were more than curious about

al-Mansur and Morocco: They were rivals and potential enemies (or, in the diplomatic setting of the time, secret allies). One
account written in 1591 is a rich if short report from an author
who is known today as the Anonymous Spaniard (his identity
has never been satisfactorily established). This individual was in
Marrakesh in some official capacity for the Spanish government, but actually he was a covert agent. His report includes
highly confidential information on military matters relating to
al-Mansur's invasion of the Songhay Empire. Obviously his
contacts included officials high in the Moroccan government.

A recently discovered manuscript by a Portuguese captive,
António de Saldanha, is proving to be a valuable source of information. The son of the Portuguese governor of Tangier, de
Saldanha was captured in battle in 1592 and held in Marrakesh
for fourteen years. Allowed considerable freedom of movement
within the capital, he came to know high-ranking officials and
other important people. His account begins with the events
leading up to Wadi al-Makhazin, and somewhat less than half
of the book concerns the period before he arrived as a captive.
He is interested in political and diplomatic history, particularly
matters involving Spain, and occasionally he provides valuable
economic information. For events outside Marrakesh, his accuracy varies according to his source. He gives a detailed account
of the Mauritanian expedition, for example, but the worst part
of his book is on the invasion and conquest of Songhay. He
provides many insights into Ahmad al-Mansur the man, whom
he alternately finds admirable and appalling.

On the other side of the geopolitical fence from the Anonymous Spaniard and António de Saldanha, the Turkish historian
Mustafa al-Jannabi wrote a massive history of the Islamic
world, *Al-Bakr al-Zakhar*, which covers eighty-two dynasties
including those of Morocco. The section on the Sa'dis appears
reasonably well balanced with positive and negative comments,
and it is especially generous in characterizing al-Mansur. Nevertheless, al-Jannabi leaves no doubt that the Ottoman Empire
and its sultan were preeminent over places like Morocco and
rulers like al-Mansur. Al-Jannabi's work, completed around
1587, covers only the beginning of al-Mansur's reign.

The last source of note was written about a century and a half after al-Mansur's death, but it follows up on his legacy in the Western Sudan. The anonymous *Tedzkiret en-Nisian* is a biographical dictionary of the Moroccan and Arma pashas of Timbuktu, arranged alphabetically (by the Arabic alphabet). It makes no attempt to tell a story and offers no analysis or explanation of events. Occasionally, categorical statements or sweeping generalizations appear out of nowhere, with no supporting evidence. The *Tedzkiret* is much harder to use than any of the previously mentioned works, but despite its many annoyances it is a mine of information for those patient enough to tunnel into it.

VI

The Invasion of Songhay

Late in 1589, Ahmad al-Mansur was in Fez when he received a letter from one Wuld Kirinfil, who had recently arrived in Marrakesh. This person claimed to be the reigning Askiya's elder brother, Ali, who had once been ruler of Songhay but had been overthrown and unjustly imprisoned in Taghaza. The letter claimed that the Songhay were in a deplorable condition "because of the baseness of their nature" and the state was weak from the Balama's rebellion. Wuld Kirinfil implored the sultan to champion his cause, "to seize the country and tear it out of the hands of its masters." Conquering Songhay would be "something very simple," and he promised to give al-Mansur rich treasure and serve as his tributary.

Much speculation has been made about the real identity of Wuld Kirinfil, who, all sources except al-Fishtali agree, was not a Songhay prince. Evidence seems to indicate he was a royal slave, probably born and raised in the Askiya's palace, who had "shown himself to be so wicked and debauched," as the Anonymous Spaniard put it, that he was imprisoned in Taghaza. Apparently with the connivance of the local governor, he escaped and somehow made his way to Marrakesh.

When Wuld Kirinfil's letter reached him, al-Mansur was in the middle of some nasty business involving the *shurafa* of Fez. They had recently committed an act of rebellion, for which al-Mansur had ordered them to be blinded—an operation carried out with such brutality that many of them died. Al-Sadi claims that the sultan did this because he begrudged their wealth, which he then confiscated.

Wuld Kirinfil's letter was a godsend. Al-Mansur must have known that Wuld Kirinfil was an imposter, but he could be used as a pretext for reopening the question of Taghaza and for probing larger issues concerning Songhay. With this in mind, in December 1589, al-Mansur sent his own letter to the reigning Askiya, Ishaq II, notifying him that the salt mine at Taghaza (by which he could have meant either Taghaza or Taoudeni) "is in our domain and under the rule of our imamate." It was to be used to provide income for the Treasury of All the Muslims, which was conveniently located in Marrakesh, "in pursuit of campaigning and jihad" against the "infidel enemies of God." The sultan informed the Askiya that he had sought a *fatwa*, a legal opinion, on the question of the mines, from experts in Islamic law "who told him that under strict law the disposition of the mines belonged to the single chief of the Muslim community and not to others. No one could thus exploit a mine without the authority of the sultan or of his representative."

Islamic society was based on law, and the issuance of *fatwas* was the most important function of legal scholars known as muftis. They were the final arbiters of Islamic law (*shari'a*), and rulers took their opinions very seriously. Normally *fatwas* were not rubberstamps, although those who rendered them generally did not make a point of defying their rulers. This particular *fatwa* was issued by jurisconsults from the Marrakesh region who were in the habit of supporting the Sa'di ruler, and given what had just happened to the *shurafa* of Fez, they were likely to agree with al-Mansur in whatever he wanted. To appear magnanimous to the Askiya, al-Mansur agreed to leave the mine in the hands of the Songhay for the time being. He would, however, take a tax of one mithqal per camel load to go to the Treasury of All Muslims. Al-Mansur included a copy of the *fatwa* and of Wuld Kirinfil's letter and assured the Askiya that "your brother" was being given hospitality "in our noble prophetic sanctuary." The sultan would await the Askiya's reply before considering Wuld Kirinfil's request for support.

A second undated letter from around this time addressed to Askiya Ishaq II, which some scholars think was really meant for Mai Idris Aloma of Bornu, provides insight into the caliph's state of mind. It refers to his attempt at "persuasion before threatening with the clash of mounted men." He summons his reader "to contract a debt with God through the obligation of obedience to us, and through entering into the bond of allegiance to us, which the community of Muslims has entered into." Later he mentions, in Qur'anic language, "this holy imamate, whose lights have spread across the eastern and western lands, and have traveled over its lowlands and its highlands." He orders "that you should obey his [the Prophet Muhammad's] noble commands in regard to that complete obedience that God has imposed toward this Prophetic caliphate." The temper of this letter is at the same time mystical and overbearingly imperious. In al-Mansur's mind the caliphate had become far more than a propaganda device or a tool for browbeating; it was an obsession.

His affairs in Fez settled, al-Mansur set out for Marrakesh in midwinter 1590, not the best time to cross the Atlas Mountains. His entourage was caught in a blizzard in which the sultan nearly froze to death, and many of his companions lost hands and feet from frostbite. He was not in a good mood when he arrived in Marrakesh to find Ishaq's reply, a letter scoffing at the demand for the salt mine, accompanied by javelins and two iron shoes, meant as a challenge and an insult. The Songhay were probably tired of trying to placate the insatiable Moroccans; it was time to call the Sa'di bluff. Al-Mansur is said to have "become furious," according to al-Fishtali. Al-Sadi notes that "as soon as this message reached him, Ahmad al-Mansur decided to send an army to the Sudan." His motive, al-Ifrani observes, was as old and as simple as human aggression: "Master of the countries of Tuwat and Tigourarin and of their dependencies, al-Mansur dreamed of conquering the Sudan, which now bordered his new possessions." No doubt Ishaq's response was intended to offend al-Mansur, but the report that the sultan flew into a rage and suddenly ordered an invasion seems stretched. Al-Zayyani believes he had been methodically and systematically preparing to send such an expedition for three years.

If al-Mansur, from his position as Commander of the Faithful, decided to invade Songhay for a mixture of religious, political, and economic reasons, he could justify it only on the purest of grounds, that of religion. The Songhay were vulnerable on one enormous issue. Only a small portion, albeit the elite of this society, was Muslim, and the Islam that most of them practiced was syncretic, a blend of Islamic and local beliefs and practices that was corrupt by the standards of an orthodox North African. The people who lived in the Songhay Empire were still largely animists and polytheists—in short, pagans. It could be argued that those responsible for ensuring the quality of the One True Religion in the Western Sudan, the Songhay rulers, had done badly enough to warrant their overthrow. Jihads had often been aimed at fellow Muslims when their brand of Islam was corrupt or diluted.

Al-Mansur, however, did not use the argument against a corrupt Islam in legitimatizing his plans. Rather, he maintained that invading the Western Sudan was a crucial step in the jihad against the Christians. With the wealth of the Western Sudan, the Moroccans would be able to invade the Iberian peninsula and reestablish the faith there; the road to Cordoba lay through Timbuktu. And an unlimited supply of Sudanese gold would allow the Commander of the Faithful to bring the Islamic world together and prepare it for the millennial apocalypse. Al-Mansur's messianic mission gave him the right to conquer other Muslims. The Songhay would benefit from a change of leadership by coming under the Prophet's true heir and thus would live under Divine Guidance. Far from oppressing his fellow Africans, al-Mansur saw himself as a true African hero in the struggle to expel foreign devils, the Portuguese, Spanish, and Turks.

Despite this justification, al-Mansur did not initially enjoy widespread support for his Songhay project. The failure of the Mauritania and Taghaza expeditions had produced dissatisfaction, and within the government the general feeling was that an attack on Songhay would be too risky and too expensive. Military leaders were concerned about strategic considerations—specifically, how to get an army across the desert. More annoying was the skepticism bordering on outright criticism from the religious establishment, which was supposed to be the Sa'dis' source of strength. The learned and holy communities of Morocco, including the ulama of Marrakesh and Fez, were concerned that al-Mansur would be judged a tyrant if he invaded brother Muslims when there were infidels nearby to attack. And his transgression would be greater for using Islamic solidarity as a rationale for what could be seen as unprovoked aggression.

To the sultan's ulama critics, war was a moral question, and righteous war meant jihad against the Christians. War against the Ottomans might be allowed on grounds of self-defense or perhaps over the question of who was the rightful leader of Islam, but war against the Songhay would not please God. Unlike the Ottoman Empire, Songhay was no danger to Morocco. The Songhay, as the Anonymous Chronicler of Fez put it, were "innocents." Furthermore, the Askiya dynasty had been given legitimacy when the last Abbasid caliph bestowed the title of *khalifa* on Askiya Muhammad, making him deputy over West Africa. Al-Ifrani admits that this act "delegated to him authority over the affairs of those regions and made him his lieutenant over the Muslims," and this distinction had been passed down to Askiya Muhammad's heirs. Al-Mansur could not refute this line of reasoning, so he ignored it.

To swing public opinion in favor of his proposed invasion, al-Mansur called a council of notables, a consultative assembly composed of the most respected ulama, the highest military commanders, and other "men of judgment." To this august body he laid out his plan, expecting an outburst of approval. He was greeted with silence. When he asked what was wrong, the braver spokesmen articulated their concerns. Whether al-Mansur intended it that way or not, the affair concluded in his favor by allowing him a forum in which to address each objection with an effective counterargument.

Al-Mansur's line of reasoning began with this assumption: He was the caliph divinely ordained to unite Islam and spread it over the earth. He intended to begin with the reconquest of Andalusia, but he needed the wealth of the Western Sudan to accomplish this. Therefore, whoever criticized his campaign against the Songhay was opposing the reestablishment of Islam on the Iberian peninsula. That settled, much of the discussion turned on practical matters. Al-Mansur scorned the idea that an army could not make it across the desert: "You talk of the dangerous desert we have to cross . . . but you forget the defenseless and ill-equipped merchants who, mounted or on foot, regularly cross these wastes which caravans have never ceased to traverse. I, who am so much better equipped than they, can surely do the same with an army which inspires terror wherever it goes." The Songhay army would be much larger than his force. No problem; "Today the Sudanese have only spears and swords, weapons which will be useless against modern arms. It will therefore be easy for us to wage a successful war against these people and prevail over them."

The only way to refute the argument from religion was to deny that al-Mansur was the God-appointed caliph anointed to unify Islam and prepare it for the end of the world. No one chose to do this. In this heady atmosphere the sultan's enthusiasm and charisma may have raised the adrenaline level to fever pitch. Perhaps the notables were now convinced that it was not just in the interests of Morocco to conquer Songhay; it was in the interests of the whole of Islam. Far from committing aggression against fellow Muslims, the invasion of the Western Sudan was a lawful jihad because Askiya Ishaq II had taken Songhay out of the Muslim fold by refusing to submit to the orders of the caliph.

On the other hand, the ulama may have realized that their assembly was consultative, that Ahmad al-Mansur was determined to have his way in this matter, and that he was providing a salve for their collective conscience. This sultan had shown himself a great friend and benefactor of the religious and scholarly elite, and many in the ulama had been blessed by his largess. When he was finished, he asked for their approval, and he received it in full. Al-Mansur had no intention of sharing power with the religious establishment, the officer corps, or anyone else, but he wanted to give the impression that his decision came after full consultation with those whose opinions mattered. If in their hearts the ulama were never reconciled to al-Mansur's Songhay policy, as the Anonymous Chronicler of Fez claims, their opposition had no impact on subsequent developments.

The sultan had learned from the Mauritanian disaster of 1584. His new army would be smaller and have the best of everything. The troops were to be "the most valiant of the men, of which he knew of their loyalty and devotion," according to al-Ifrani. The Anonymous Spaniard maintains that the invading force consisted of one thousand renegade and one thousand Andalusian infantry musketeers, five hundred mounted muske-teers, fifteen hundred lancers drawn from the most loyal Moroccan tribes, and one thousand support personnel. Al-Sadi gives a figure of three thousand arquebusiers, mounted and on foot, and Mahmud Kati quotes numbers that vary between three and four thousand.

Command was given to Judar (Jawdar) Pasha, described by al-Sadi as short and having blue eyes. According to Spanish sources, he was born in Las Cuevas in Granada to Christian parents, captured as a boy by Barbary corsairs, made a eunuch, and raised as a royal slave in the palace at Marrakesh. António de Saldanha agrees that Judar was a renegade and a eunuch but claims he was born in Tangier and implies he was of Portuguese origin. Having eunuchs was a symbol of prestige; in some places only rulers were allowed to own them. A eunuch, their masters typically assumed, could be trusted more fully than other men: He had nothing to secure, no family to inherit his goods or titles, no interests in life beyond serving his master. Often eunuchs rose to powerful positions running the inner workings of royal households, where they had access to confi-dential information. They were thought to be a good counter-balance to officials whose positions depended on birth and property, including princes of the blood.

According to the Anonymous Spaniard, Judar had never ex-perienced all-out warfare but had distinguished himself in the effective use of force to collect the sultan's taxes. António de Saldanha maintains he was one of the renegades elevated to high position, with the title qa'id of the qa'ids at the beginning of al-Mansur's reign when Andalusian leaders fell from favor. Judar was chosen to lead the expedition because of his energy, organizational talent, and unflinching loyalty. His title of pasha, borrowed from the Turks, signified both viceroy and supreme military commander. Judar's force was divided into ten battalions, each commanded by a qa'id, and was grouped into right and left wings, each commanded by a lieutenant qa'id. Wuld Kirinfil, the would-be brother of the Askiya, would serve

Photo 6.1 Landscape Between Arawan and the Niger. Courtesy of author.

as chief guide. Supplies were carried on the backs of more than ten thousand camels selected for their strength and vigor and a thousand horses to be used later as mounts in battle. Among the ordnance packed away were four small cannons and ten mortars, according to the Anonymous Spaniard (who gives slightly different figures in another place). The expedition left Marrakesh on October 25, 1590, with much pomp, "a vast parade and an unprecedented spectacle," according to al-Ifrani. It was the final year of the first millennium of the hijra.

Judar followed the ancient gold route southeast, stopping briefly at Taghaza and Taoudeni before hurrying on, leaving behind the dead and the dying at a rate that evened out to about one per mile. During the crossing the Moroccans were vulnerable to attack from desert warriors, but none came. The Tuaregs had sided with the forces of the west during the revolt of the Balama, and their high chief had been among those executed; they remained sullen and resentful and did not so much as harass Judar. When the Moroccans reached Arawan, the oasis marking the southern reaches of the Sahara, they detoured to avoid setting off an alarm, pausing only long enough to confiscate camels from a local herder, Abd Allah b. Qair al-Mahmudi. He then set off for Marrakesh, where, between his bitter complaints and demands for compensation, Ahmad al-Mansur received confirmation that Judar's army had almost made it across the Sahara.

The expedition reached the Niger River between Timbuktu and Gao on March 1, 1591, according to Mahmud Kati (who is probably correct); al-Sadi puts the arrival at the end of March, and al-Ifrani has it in February. Only about half of Judar's men survived; the rest had died of sunstroke, freezing night air, dehydration, or fatigue. But the Songhay were not waiting to do battle. Ishaq II had been preparing for a campaign on the upper Niger, clear across the empire from where Judar's army emerged, and the Songhay army lay scattered between Gao and Ishaq's planned point of attack.

The Askiya had been given hints that something was afoot in the north, but he did not appreciate the gravity of the situation. In August, two months before Judar set out, Ahmad al-Mansur sent a letter to the Qadi of Timbuktu, Umar b. Mahmud, in an attempt to sway the ulama of that city. The sultan began by bemoaning the "task whose necklace has been hung upon our noble neck," a reference to his leadership over all of Islam. He mentions "the first and last of us," meaning the Prophet Muhammad and the Mahdi, implying that he was the latter. Since he was of the Prophet's blood, "God appointed us to the Great Imamate [and] through it made unquestioning obedience to us binding upon people." In other words, this was all God's doing, and God would accept no excuses. Al-Mansur was merely His instrument, but one that could bring horrible chastisement to those who resisted: "Our soldiers whose firearms are like the deafening rumble from the end of the world will conquer the land, region by region, until we will have seized your borders."

Al-Mansur was a frequent letter writer who always wrote with a purpose. Having had no success in dealing directly with Ishaq, the sultan hoped to persuade other influential men, particularly those associated with religion and law, who themselves might have influence on the government in Gao. If not, it would be helpful once the sultan's army reached Songhay to have the religious establishment sympathetic to his cause. But he probably underestimated Umar b. Mahmud. The qadi and the cadre of intellectuals who gathered around the schools of higher education in Timbuktu were hardly bumpkins waiting on the far edge of the Islamic world to be awed by claims of Mahdihood, the Great Imamate, and the Prophetic Caliphate. They knew that from a doctrinal point of view al-Mansur's self-proclaimed role in the world of Islam was shaky, and for the time being the new caliph's power stopped more than a thousand miles to the north. Qadi Umar probably turned the letter over to the Askiya or his officials or at least shared its contents. Yet no one seems to have paid much attention; the Songhay believed the desert would protect their land from an army large enough to threaten it.

Judar's arrival caught the government in Gao off guard. The Askiya summoned a council of army officers, government officials, and wise and important men: "Each time a judicious counsel was given," al-Sadi reports, "they hastened to reject it. God, in his foresight, had decided that this kingdom would disappear and that this dynasty would collapse." Askiya Ishaq II had become weak and indecisive. And increasingly he appears to have been under the influence of Bukar Lanbaru, the imperial secretary, who handled all of the Askiya's diplomatic and internal correspondence and the promulgation of edicts. In addition, Bukar served as the personal chaplain of the Askiya. He was also one of the greatest operatives of all time, a deeply placed mole in the service of Ahmad al-Mansur. Bukar Lanbaru's motives are hazy. He may have been sincerely convinced that the Moroccans were sent by God to cleanse the land and punish the Songhay for their sins, or he may have been a traitor in the pay of the sultan. In either case, his influence would be decisive. As information about Judar arrived, the imperial secretary made sure that the inner circles of government remained paralyzed for as long as possible.

The Songhay Empire had never before been invaded and only rarely been raided. Its leaders had no experience in dealing with such a situation and had planned no contingencies. The imperial Songhay army was a professional force whose soldiers constituted a privileged class but were legally the Askiya's slaves (so that the Askiya inherited their property when they died). Thus a soldier could accumulate wealth only by merit, which meant audacity to the point of foolhardiness. The infantry were armed largely with bows and arrows tipped with poison and were protected by shields made of leather. For close fighting they used cudgels and bludgeons. Leading the infantry were the Sunna, an elite corps of Sudanese Praetorian Guards distinguished by their armlets of gold, who took an oath to fight to the death. The cavalry was recruited from the warrior nobility, again with reckless bravery, the surest avenue up the ranks of the officer corps. Cavalrymen carried quivers full of short javelins, which they hurled with speed and accuracy. Otherwise, they fought in the medieval knight fashion with lances and swords. A typical battle opened with a missile exchange, but shock tactics usually decided the day. In a pitched battle on an open field, nothing in West Africa could withstand a cavalry charge, although poison-tipped arrows could do considerable damage to the horses.

The Songhay army was an imposing but traditional force compared to that of the Moroccans. Songhay formations and tactics were still based on the mob theory of warfare. The infantry moved into battle behind standards and typically fought in a fan-shaped formation, with orders conveyed by the blowing of horns. At the outset of a battle soldiers fired their arrows until a signal was given to charge. This was done en masse, and the result was a melee. None of the wealth the Songhay state had generated through trade and taxes had been used to modernize the army, and the Songhay had made no attempt to move into the era of gunpowder weapons and disciplined formations. Perhaps they had not considered this to be necessary; the major threat had always come from within. The Songhay believed that no outside force in West Africa could threaten their power—a situation that bred lethargy and carelessness.

The Songhay army was recalled, and it assembled outside the town of Tondibi, twenty-seven miles north of Gao, on the left bank of the river. When Judar learned of this, he sent a message to Ishaq appealing to the Askiya to submit freely to the sultan, "seeing that he was a sharif, a descendant of the Prophet, and to him legitimately belonged sovereignty over all the Muslims." In return the Askiya would receive many honors and favors. The offer was dismissed. In Moroccan eyes the Songhay had now forfeited their status as true Muslims because they had refused to recognize Ahmad al-Mansur as the Imam. They had made themselves deserving of death.

The Battle of Tondibi is one of those historical events reported on by a limited number of sources who appear to be in almost total disagreement on specific factual information. The date it was fought is put by al-Ifrani at February 16, by Mahmud Kati at March 12, and by al-Sadi at April 12, 1591. Reports on the size of the Songhay army range from al-Fishtali's outrageous figure of 104,000, to the Anonymous Spaniard's curious proviso that it "could have been more than 80,000," to al-Sadi's claims of 30,000 infantry and 12,500 cavalry, to Mahmud Kati's awkward figures of 18,000 cavalry and 9,700 infantry. The most reasonable estimate is that of al-Sadi. Ahmad al-Mansur later boasted that "their number was so great that one imagined the gathering of humanity on Judgment Day," and so it probably seemed to the Moroccan soldiers on the field.

The precise location of the battlefield has not been identified, but it had to be along the Niger because both armies positioned their troops in relation to the river. The Anonymous Spaniard maintains that the battle lasted for two hours. Al-Sadi, who provides no tactical details, observes in rather cavalier fashion that it was over "in the twinkling of an eye." Al-Ifrani seems at first to agree, noting that "when the two armies met, Ishaq saw that all was lost and turned his heels and his troops dispersed." That this was not the case is attested by al-Ifrani himself, who in another passage states that the battle lasted from mid-morning to mid-afternoon, which is the time al-Zayyani gives as well.

On one matter all sources agree: Judar's much smaller force defeated Ishaq's much larger force by blasting it to smithereens. Given its enormous consequences, Tondibi may be one of the most under-noticed battles in world history, but when it is studied, it is generally used as an example of a classic guns-versus-spears contest. Certainly Ahmad al-Mansur had predicated his plan of invasion on the belief that firepower would more than compensate for inferior numbers. The Moroccans, however, had an additional weapon that, according to Mahmud Kati, proved to be just as effective as their muskets. While the battle raged, a major morale problem developed at Songhay headquarters as Bukar Lanbaru spread defeatism within the high command. He harangued Ishaq: "Fear God, do not go to death, do not kill your brothers and do not cause all of the Songhay to die at the same time in this one spot. God will ask you for a reckoning for the lives of all those who were killed here today for it is you who have caused their deaths if you do not flee."

At first the Askiya and his men ignored Bukar Lanbaru's pleadings, and some of the bolder chiefs plunged into the battle. In a different society one of them might have lopped off the secretary's head in passing, but among the Songhay a man of learning was considered sacrosanct. Ultimately Bukar Lanbaru grabbed the reins of the Askiya's horse and conducted him away, with the royal retinue following. Barely holding on despite the superior discipline and the deadly firepower of their enemy, Songhay soldiers watched the incredible sight of Bukar Lanbaru leading Askiya Ishaq II out of the battle. It was the final blow. The Songhay army retreated, probably in better order than could have been expected, under protection of the Sunna, who sacrificed themselves.

The Moroccans did not follow the retreat. According to al-Ifrani, they finished off those who remained behind without mercy, ignoring the cries, "We are Muslims; we are your brothers in religion." Al-Sadi describes the end of the Sunna: "When the army was defeated, the soldiers threw their shields on the ground and squatted on these improvised seats, awaiting the arrival of Judar's troops, who massacred them in this position because they could present no resistance. And that was because they must not flee in the case of a retreat by the regular army. The Moroccan soldiers stripped them of the gold bracelets they had on their arms."

A CLOSER LOOK

The Battle of Tondibi

If conventional wisdom dictates that guns will defeat spears, at Tondibi the matter was less apparent. Shooting an arquebus was an operation that required a number of steps, including a thorough cleaning after each firing. The reload time was about two minutes of interminable fumbling in the middle of a raging battle. Too often something went wrong and the gun misfired, in which case the arquebusier had to start all over again. An arquebus was no rapid-fire weapon; an experienced archer would have a much higher rate of discharge.

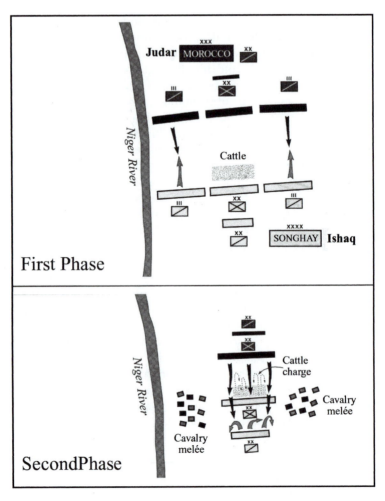

Figure 6.2   The Battle of Tondibi. Courtesy of Routledge Press, 1999.

Firearms, however, had significant advantages. The three-quarter-inch lead ball an arquebus discharged could penetrate armor, and in Europe the new weapon closed the era of the medieval knight. The Songhay cavalry at Tondibi had armor and chain mail, and the Songhay nobility would also fade into oblivion. In descriptions of Tondibi, however, the crushing blow seems to have come against the Songhay infantry, which could fire its arrows faster than the musketeers could shoot. The great advantage the Moroccans had was in massed fire-power from a disciplined formation, the kind of instant devastation that mows down entire lines of an advancing enemy. If maintaining a constant rate of fire using the volley technique was still a few years away (it was introduced in 1594 by the Dutch), Moroccan tactics at Tondibi appear to have produced a similar effect. Two thousand arquebusiers on foot and five hundred on horseback represented a formidable amount of firepower that was the decisive consideration.

An equal if less tangible factor was the psychological one. The Songhay could not have been mentally and emotionally prepared to stand in the face of powder weapons. The booming of cannons and the crack of musket fire reverberating across the field in salvos had to be deafening and disorienting. Smoke enveloped the men, and the acrid smell of dirty powder filled every lung. To say the experience was horrifying would be an understatement.

Despite the terror, however, the Songhay did not break. In a letter of Ahmad al-Mansur, drawn from accounts he received from his officers, he notes: "The battle was engaged, the thundering of our cannons rumbled, shaking the horizon; but the accursed blacks were no more shaken than the mountains, [and] they continued their efforts at combat. . . . They knew neither fear nor fright and threw themselves from all sides on the fire from our arms like moths on a lamp." According to the Anonymous Spaniard, when Judar's forces attacked at the beginning of the engagement, the Songhay "did not refuse to fight but received the onslaught valiantly." He uses that word again in describing the action at a later point, reporting that "the Blacks fought valiantly, despite the fact that many of them fell under the musket fire." He maintains that the most valiant were the Sunna, who set an example of courage at the onset of the battle by lashing their upper and lower legs together in a kneeling position so they could not retreat.

The Anonymous Spaniard and Mahmud Kati both provide descriptions of the action, and although they are quite different in detail, their general outlines are similar. Both agree that Judar put the renegades on his right and the Andalusians on his left. The pasha himself was in the center with the rest of the troops, according to the Anonymous Spaniard, except for a large portion of the cavalry, which was positioned in the rear to defend the munitions.

Both sources have the Moroccans initiating the action. According to Mahmud Kati, five hundred cavalry from both flanks charged the enemy, and a struggle ensued. In the center the Moroccan arquebusiers dropped to one knee and fired a volley, spreading smoke across the battlefield and throwing panic into the ranks of the Songhay. As his men pulled back, Ishaq gave orders to send a thousand head of cattle straight at the Moroccans, hoping this would break their formation or at least afford his infantry protection until it could make hand-to-hand contact. The two sources diverge on what happened next. Mahmud Kati has the Moroccans firing into the herd, causing it to turn around and stampede back into the Songhay. The Anonymous Spaniard says that the Moroccans opened their ranks, and the cattle passed harmlessly through. In either case, the Songhay may have counted too much on the success of the cattle charge, and when it failed, they were left without a plan of action.

Following the cattle charge, the Moroccan cavalry made a flanking movement that surrounded a part of their foe. As they pushed into the heart of the enemy, they ran into the Sunna, who stopped them with a flurry of arrows. The Songhay were not yet finished. Although by this time their formation was likely in tatters, they counterattacked, penetrating so far into the Moroccan right they took a renegade standard. This last great charge, probably led by the reserve cavalry, further compromised the Songhay position in the face of the rigidly disciplined Moroccans, who held their lines intact. Al-Sadi makes one simple and seemingly offhand comment, but it probably explains the Songhay defeat as well as any: "The troops were not well organized."

VII

The Aftermath of Victory: Wealth and Woes

No one counted the bodies at Tondibi. The Songhay army was damaged but not destroyed, and it would return to the field for subsequent battles. Nevertheless Tondibi was decisive. Great battles are defined as turning points in history, often signaling the rise of a great state or the beginning of a notable era. Not Tondibi. It is best seen as one of the great defeats in history, the end rather than the beginning for West Africa. For Sultan Ahmad al-Mansur, Tondibi seemed an even greater victory than Wadi al-Makhazin because it was thought to have opened the door to a limitless supply of wealth. Old problems, however, are rarely solved without creating new ones, and Tondibi, as al-Mansur would soon discover, would not even solve the old problems.

As Ishaq II retreated with the main body of his army, he sent evacuation orders to the inhabitants of Gao. The result was a disaster. Mobs scrambled aboard the available boats, many of which were swamped: "In the scuffle that took place," al-Sadi observes, "many people fell in the river and perished. Further-more such a quantity of wealth was lost that only God knows its value." Shortly afterward the victorious army entered a nearly vacant Gao, where the gold and other wealth had been removed, leaving nothing to plunder. Judar was bitterly disappointed. Gao was not built of gold or even stone and marble, as were the great cities of Morocco, but of mudbrick. A visit to the palace, which he claims to have found "rather miserable," compounded his disillusionment. To Ahmad al-Mansur he wrote: "The house of the shaykh of the donkey drivers in Morocco was worth more than the Askiya's palace."

Facing a disappointed Judar from across the river was a despondent Askiya Ishaq II. Had he been able to reorganize the Songhay army and counterattack, he might have been successful. But Tondibi was a shock Ishaq never got over. He had lost all confidence in himself and his army; more important, he had lost the will to mobilize his nation and drive out the invaders. The Moroccans, he decided, could have whatever they wanted. He sent an emissary to Judar offering the sultan his submission plus a hundred thousand mithqals of gold, a thousand slaves, and the right to export salt to Songhay tariff-free if the Moroccans would go home.

Judar liked the idea. Instead of a terrestrial paradise, the Moroccans found themselves in an unhealthy climate. Many of the men and most of the animals had already contracted one of the diseases that lurk in the riverain tropics, and they were dying in alarming numbers. The army shared Judar's attitude. They were mercenaries: They had come, they had conquered, and now it was time to take what they could and go. Judar replied to Ishaq that he was "only a docile slave" and could not act without orders from the sovereign, his master. However, he would recommend that Ishaq's offer be accepted. The Askiya then suggested that while they were awaiting the sultan's reply, the Moroccans would find the desert climate of Timbuktu more salubrious, and he offered to supply horses to help them move. Judar accepted.

At Timbuktu the people led by Qadi Umar were uncooperative. Judar presented a letter from the sultan that praised the qadi and at the same time threatened him if he did not cooperate. Umar seemed unmoved. When the qadi ignored Judar's request for space in the city to billet his troops and store his gunpowder, the Moroccans marched into the city and confiscated a rich, densely inhabited neighborhood, evicting the residents and tearing down their great homes to create a casbah, a walled citadel from which the Moroccans could dominate Timbuktu. Then Judar slapped a "contribution" on the city's merchants, which obligated them to provision his army. The qadi's protests were ignored. In Timbuktu the ulama were no longer in charge.

Victory Celebration

In Marrakesh, Sultan Ahmad al-Mansur awaited news of his great venture. He was now spending much of his time in semi-seclusion in the yet-to-be completed Badi palace, where he managed much of the day-to-day affairs of the realm. He kept his secretaries busy with a stream of correspondence to his governors and other functionaries, ordering and advising them on a variety of matters. He also sent out brave messages to be read by the imams of important mosques during the sermon that accompanied the Friday midday prayer. In these messages he referred to his forces as representing the armies of God and those of the Songhay the armies of Satan. And his propaganda machine was proposing new conquests. He would take the holy cities of Mecca and Medina under his protection, which would signal his domination over the entire Muslim world. He would conquer "the East" as far as the Indies.

Al-Mansur had instituted new ceremonies and rituals, including the practice of having his hand kissed. When he went out, he rode in a solemn manner with a parasol held high over his head, which was said to symbolize nearness to God. On Fridays he would dress in white robes and ride through the streets with much pomp to the city's main mosque, one servant holding the parasol and another fanning him with white ostrich feathers. Occasionally he would venture out of Marrakesh to lead military processions and parades, sometimes in conjunction with the crown prince. Early in 1589 al-Mansur had made a tour of the country between Marrakesh and Fez, accompanied by his army. In Fez he made a grand entry, riding in the middle of his soldiers under the shade of the largest of his parasols and surrounded by the fluttering white flags of his dynasty. Such displays when done right—and Ahmad al-Mansur was a master—were sixteenth-century public relations extravaganzas. An Ottoman embassy that happened to be in Fez at the time of his entry was ushered to the roof of a building so it could have the best view in town.

When Judar's messengers arrived with news of the victory at Tondibi along with Ishaq's offer and Judar's recommendation, al-Mansur ordered three days of celebration. The streets of Marrakesh were lined with flags, and people paraded about rejoicing "because of the massacre of human creatures who were Muslims," as the Anonymous Chronicler of Fez put it sourly. Delegations arrived: "He received ambassadors from all sides who came to congratulate him on his triumph and on the brilliant success that God had procured for his armies," the more cheery al-Ifrani notes. Speeches were given and poems written to celebrate the glorious triumph, including one by the ever slavish al-Fishtali:

> The army of the day charged the army of the night,
>
> And the oncoming whiteness extinguished the blackness.
>
> The standards of your army were raised above the blacks
>
> And their white mass floated brilliantly across that horizon of darkness
>
> Just like a ray of dawn that cuts into the obscurity of night. . . .
>
> The darkness of the night was dissipated before them
>
> Thanks to the prophetic halo that gleamed on your front.

Letters announcing the victory began with praise for the Quraysh tribe and al-Mansur's holy dynasty, "the guide of mankind." This victory was said to be an important step in uniting Islam. It was, of course, dutifully credited to God, or as al-Mansur explained, "God made the wind of victory and glory blow," but also to the "Slave of God who fights on the path of God," as al-Mansur styled himself. He claimed to have taken Islam to the Songhay—the fact that the Songhay royal family had officially been Muslim for more than five centuries was appropriately forgotten—and the Songhay were said to have been invaded and slaughtered because they were the "unbelieving enemy." Victory in battle, particularly in jihad, was another sign of a caliph.

Earlier, in trying to arouse support for his venture, al-Mansur had understated the difficulties his men would encounter and the dangers they would face. Now he exaggerated them to magnify the scope of his triumph. The desert crossing was hailed as an almost superhuman achievement, and the Songhay army was portrayed as enormous and savagely ferocious. The Niger was compared in its wealth to "the river of heaven." Al-Fishtali

Photo 7.1 "The River of Heaven." The Niger, seen here at low season, was the lifeblood of the Western Sudan. Courtesy of author.

reported that the sultan's power reached from Morocco across the Sahara and the Western Sudan to Nubia on the southern border of Egypt. Even if Bornu was included, this was an excessively inflated claim, but at the moment no one seemed to mind. Al-Ifrani, usually more temperate, was carried away: "It was an immense kingdom and a powerful empire, such that no one before him had possessed anything like it."

Others saw portents converging. Al-Mansur had built an African empire to challenge the Ottoman Empire, and a true caliphate had arisen in the west that had swept south and would soon turn north and east. The conquest of Songhay was a sign that the coming of the Redeemer was imminent. All the millennial traditions maintained that there would be signs, but their nature and the timing involved were subject to interpretation. Many believed the situation would be clarified by the revelation of secret predictions. If indeed the Mahdi had come, the appearance of al-Dajjal, the Antichrist, could not be far behind; according to one tradition, only seven years would separate the two. Other traditions foretold one hundred years of calamities before Judgment Day, although, in general, calamities were more common in Christian than in Islamic eschatology. The sun would rise in the west, and there would be two great blowings of heavenly trumpets, separated by forty years. On the second blowing the dead would rise and the world would end.

Pashas and Askiyas Come and Go

As the faithful waited for someone with irrefutable holy credentials to proclaim Ahmad al-Mansur the Mahdi, al-Mansur himself was busy with practical concerns. If he was delighted that his troops had won the Battle of Tondibi, he was enraged about everything else in Judar's letter. The Askiya's proposal was an insult, and the Songhay were in no position to offer a deal. According to al-Fishtali, Al-Mansur was so insightful he could see from across the desert that Ishaq was stalling for time in order to rebuild his army—a ploy that Judar, who was on the scene, was unable to detect. Judar had been sent to conquer Songhay, not to negotiate with the enemy; he had not captured the Askiya, and he had not sent back the gold the sultan greedily awaited. To have conquered Gao and then abandoned it was in direct violation of his orders, which had instructed Judar to build a fort there.

For his failure and his presumption, Judar would be replaced by someone more determined and aggressive, someone who shared al-Mansur's grand vision of empire. Such a man was Mahmud b. Zarqun, a royal eunuch who had risen to become qa'id of the renegade division, making him the second highest ranking officer in the Moroccan army. He was appointed pasha and sent south with orders to destroy Ishaq's force, conquer West Africa, and drain its riches.

According to the Anonymous Spaniard, the sultan was already planning to penetrate the lands beyond Songhay, "to discover other countries and make new conquests." Judar was to stay and assist the new pasha in the war effort, but he was to be demoted. In his own hand, the sultan wrote Judar: "Would you offer me money? What God has given me is better than what He has given you, though you rejoice in your gift. Return to them [the Songhay]. We shall come to them with armies they have no power against and we shall expel them from [their lands] in a state of humiliation and abasement."

Judar's replacement, Mahmud b. Zarqun, was energetic, tenacious, and ruthless, Sultan al-Mansur's tool of wrath. Al-Mansur knew how to choose men, and in his own way Mahmud b. Zarqun was as capable as Judar. Judar was more cunning, more pragmatic, less taut; despite his many excesses, he appears more human. Mahmud Pasha seems rigidly one dimensional, an easy man to hate. Accompanied by his second-in-command, Qa'id Mami b. Barrun, and a small bodyguard, Mahmud Pasha traveled across the Sahara in the dead of summer, arriving in Timbuktu on August 17.

Under its new command, the Moroccan army set off for its second encounter with the Songhay, leaving behind a garrison in Timbuktu. On October 14, five days before the year 1000 in the Muslim calendar was to begin, the Moroccans met the Songhay outside the town of Bamba and routed them. The Songhay fled, and the Moroccans followed looking for a knockout blow. Meanwhile, in Timbuktu the attitude of the city's populace had become surlier. When the Moroccan army marched out on the Bamba campaign, radical elements began plotting an uprising. On the morning of October 19, at the onset of the new millennium, the city took up arms. For the next two months the Moroccans were besieged by bow-wielding militiamen who dominated the city's rooftops. No estimate exists of how many townsfolk perished, but the Moroccans carefully counted their dead: seventy-six soldiers and the would-be Askiya Wuld Kirinfil. When the time came, they intended to exact the maximum retribution.

On hearing of the garrison's predicament, Mahmud Pasha was furious. On December 7 he wrote to the qadi, holding him accountable for the uprising. While the lower classes were doubtless "seduced by the demons that [served as] agents of the rebellious and evil Askiya," their betters were expected to keep these matters in check: "In brief, of this affair, it is you who carries all this responsibility . . . because you know what are your responsibilities under Allah, powerful and great, and because you know also what will happen to the one who disrupts the pact with the prophetic house, that is to say, Our Master Abu

Photo 7.2 On day one of the new millennium A.H., Timbuktu rose against the Moroccans. For two months bow-wielding militiamen dominated the city's rooftops. Courtesy of author.

l'Abbas al-Mansur." The pasha informed the qadi that he was sending four hundred arquebusiers to reestablish order, but the Moroccans would be conciliatory in their treatment of the city. In fact, Mahmud Pasha informed Qa'id Mami that once the city had been pacified, his troops would have seven days to engage in *sebil*, a license given to soldiers by the sultan to massacre, rape, and commit whatever atrocities they wished against a rebellious town. Sebil was usually proclaimed for one or two days; a seven-day sebil was a death sentence for any town.

Fortunately for Timbuktu, Mami had other ideas. A realistic and intelligent man who saw beyond the short-range policies that would ruin the Western Sudan, Mami reasoned that the sultan would get more wealth from the city by keeping it alive than by killing it. Nor did he consider the city's ulama a threat to the new empire: "The city of Timbuktu," he observed, "could not stand even an hour of sebil: the inhabitants are the most effeminate of men and the least courageous and, if you kill three of them, seven more would die of fright without steel ever having touched them." Mami reached Timbuktu in the last week of 1591, and within a few days the city had been pacified under a general pardon accompanied by an apology from the qa'id. When he saw one of his men rob a passerby on the street, Mami decapitated the soldier and set his head on a pole. Unfortunately for Timbuktu, Mami b. Barrun was not marching to the beat of his superiors, the pasha and the sultan.

Mahmud Pasha had not gone to Timbuktu himself because he and the Songhay army were chasing each other around downriver. The Moroccans had feigned a retreat, drawing the Songhay into still another bloody defeat and then massacring those Songhay soldiers who offered submission. As reported by the Anonymous Chronicler of Fez, "these unfortunate blacks, raising their hands to heaven invoked their community of religion; but the barbarians [Mahmud Pasha's men] continued the butchery." The Moroccans were estimated to have killed ten times their own number. Then they marched north, massacring and enslaving everyone in their path.

The Songhay army had finally had enough of Ishaq, who was overthrown and replaced by another half-brother, Muhammad Gao. Ishaq fled southwestward to Gurma, one of the smaller states on the fringe of the Songhay Empire that the Songhay had frequently raided for slaves and plunder. The local king proved magnanimous, providing Ishaq with a large house, but on the night of his arrival a mob of angry townspeople attacked and knocked it down, crushing the former Askiya to death.

Back in Songhay the new Askiya, Muhammad Gao, had concluded that continued resistance was futile and the only wise course of action was to get the best terms possible from the Moroccans. He sent word to the pasha that he wanted to negotiate a peace treaty and would be willing to take the bay'a to al-Mansur. Two emissaries were sent to make the arrangements, the Hi-koy, the highest ranking military officer in the Songhay Empire, and Bukar Lanbaru, still imperial secretary, still confidante to the Askiyas, still Moroccan superagent. On their return, the suspicious Hi-koy recommended that the Askiya not go to the pasha's camp. When it was the secretary's turn to speak, he blurted out: "By God, don't keep this man waiting who to me has been nothing but just and loyal in his pledges."

The following morning the Askiya set out with an entourage of sixty-three dignitaries (or eighty-three, depending on the source). When they arrived in the Moroccan camp, the Askiya was helped off his horse by the pasha and Qa'id Mami, who had returned from Timbuktu. The delegation was escorted into tents while soldiers marched by, firing their guns in the Askiya's honor. Following a great feast, the Askiya was invited to retire to the pasha's private tent, where Mahmud and Mami presented him with a silk gown. They suggested he try it on, and when he pulled it over his head, they pounced on him, wrestled him to the ground, and tied him up with his own turban. The pasha and Mami then began yelling orders in Spanish. Strategically placed Moroccans seized the visitors' horses; others pulled up the stakes, collapsing the tents. Some of the Songhay were shot, others hacked with swords. Those who were not killed were shackled to a long chain, and the Askiya was put under guard.

Ten days later the survivors were loaded onto a boat and sent upriver to Gao with only a single soldier to watch them. Some of the Songhay plotted to overcome the guard, but the Askiya vetoed their plan. He was convinced that once al-Mansur heard what had happened, he would order them released. When they arrived in Gao, however, leg chains were put on the Askiya. Only then did he realize he was lost. The Hi-koi was crucified at the entrance to the city. Muhammad Gao and the rest of the captives were taken to a room in the palace, where they remained shackled in irons for a month before the walls were knocked down, crushing them to death. Muhammad Gao's fate had never been in doubt to anyone except himself; the decision had not been made in Gao, Timbuktu, or the pasha's camp, but in Marrakesh.

The Moroccans came to the Western Sudan believing they could simply take over the Songhay Empire. Instead they tore it down. When the Moroccans eliminated the Askiya's power, they unleashed forces that had barely been held in check by the great states of the region since the time of Ghana. With order and security gone, the Western Sudan collapsed. In the end the Moroccans had to settle for controlling the commercial lifeline that ran across the desert to Timbuktu and up and down the river between the great cities. In their view, the devil could take the rest.

How Much Wealth and for What?

For Sultan Ahmad al-Mansur, the Songhay undertaking was a high-risk, high-return venture. Initially it seemed to pay off handsomely in wealth and prestige. According to al-Ifrani, it was at this time that he received the second great appellation of al-Dhahabi, "the Golden." An English merchant who was in Marrakesh, Laurence Madoc, wrote home: "This king of Morocco is likely to be the greatest prince in the world for money, if he keeps this country." Tribute from Timbuktu was set at sixty quintals of gold a year (a quintal was about one hundred pounds), and Gao was to provide thirty mule loads of gold—all of which sounds too fantastic even for the gold-rich Western Sudan.

The wealth that flowed into the Moroccan capital was often celebrated by triumphal processions, of which al-Mansur was especially fond if foreign visitors were in attendance. Mahmud Pasha once sent back to the sultan twelve hundred young slaves, forty "loads" of gold dust, four saddles adorned with gold, "numerous loads" of ivory and ebony, pots of musk, civet cats, and other "rare and expensive items," which, according to the Anonymous Chronicler of Fez, represented only half the booty the pasha had collected. When Judar finally returned home in 1599, his triumph was recorded by another English merchant, Jasper Thomson: "He brought with him thirty camels laden with tyban, which is unrefined gold; also a great store of pepper, unicorn horns and a certain kind of wood for dyers, to some 120 camel loads; all which he presented unto the King, with 50 horses, and a great quantity of eunuchs, dwarfs, and women and men slaves, besides 15 virgins, the King of Gao's daughters, which he sendeth to be the King's concubines." Al-Ifrani refers to a "superabundance of gold" and claims that the sultan "had at the door of his palace 1,400 hammers that struck every day pieces of gold, and he had besides a quantity of the precious metal that served in the making of earrings and other jewelry." Government officials were paid in coins of pure gold: "The Moroccan sultan received so much gold that the envious were very troubled by it and the observers were very stupefied."

Much of the loot was absorbed into the state treasury to pay for al-Mansur's expanded bureaucracy and army, both of which had become enormous by Moroccan standards. But many capital improvements were made, including the construction of mosques and schools as well as the continuation of work on the Badi palace, which was finally completed in 1593. The building of fortifications was greatly expanded, particularly at the port of Larache, Sebastian's objective on his ill-fated march. For the most part, these works were monuments to the sultan's glory or instruments of his power rather than practical investment in infrastructure that would have provided returns for the Moroccan economy. The major exception to this was sugar refineries built in the Sus and near Marrakesh, which al-Zayyani described as being "as big as the pyramids." A small army of European tradesmen, principally English, were brought in to perform jobs ranging from polishing stone to making watches. More ordnance was purchased, as was nautical equipment. And not all expenditures would go for state business; the sultan made sure he treated himself. He had always been fascinated by mechanical technology, and now he set out to collect every gadget the Europeans made. He ordered the best astronomical instruments to satisfy his interest in the heavenly bodies and expensive jewelry to adorn his own body.

The Sa'di government used the great display of wealth to advance its propaganda both at home and abroad. In a letter to high personages of the realm, al-Mansur boasted of the new addition to his empire, "whose size is limitless. It is the garden of the universe. . . . Add to this the marketplaces filled with commodities and the villages that follow like pearls on a necklace. This country is a marvel that exists only in a dream." An embassy al-Mansur sent to London in 1600 bragged that the Moroccan empire in West Africa contained an astounding 86,000 cities! John Pory claims that the gold al-Mansur received from Timbuktu and Gao may have amounted to three million ducats: "Among all the princes of Africa, I supposed that there is not any one, who in richness of state, or greatness of power, may be preferred before the Zeriffo."

If al-Mansur's claims to power were so obviously exaggerated, perhaps too were his claims to the amount of wealth realized by the Songhay conquest. Camels or even donkeys laden with gold (one camel could carry up to three hundred pounds) and 1,400 hammerers turning out gold coins are statistics from the realm of fairytales. In fact, all of the evidence regarding the quantities of riches is anecdotal. Skeptics believe that the fabulous reports were largely government propaganda to hide al-Mansur's disappointment. If so, it must be admitted that his public relations men did an outstanding job. However, they could not hide several disturbing facts.

The great displays of wealth paraded through the streets of Marrakesh represented plunder, a form of income that would not last long and was not renewable. If Morocco was suddenly awash in gold, it would soon seep away, leaving the country in its former chronic fiscal straits. In West Africa the Moroccans controlled the marketplaces where the gold was brought, and al-Zayyani claims they found three gold mines near which they built a fort. If so, these deposits would prove insignificant. The Moroccans never came to within several hundred miles of the Akan goldfields. From the marketplaces the Moroccans collected duties, but too much pressure on the merchants might rupture the goose and crack the golden eggs: the more burdensome the taxes, the less profitable the business and the more likely it would fail or go elsewhere. Sultan al-Mansur tended to want cash up front and did not care about what might be ruined for the future. He probably could not have guessed it, but ultimately the most profitable economic legacy of the whole enterprise would be control of the salt trade, hardly a reason to conquer and administer an entire empire.

Beneath the self-congratulations of the sultan's court and the awe of visiting English merchants were more sober appraisals. António de Saldanha believed that despite the plunder and tribute, "they will reap nothing." The Anonymous Spaniard reports that some thought the conquest "very advantageous" for the sultan: "But those [in the Moroccan government] who consider this expedition with a saner judgment forecast that it will be the ruin of the king." The Anonymous Spaniard concludes that the invasion and occupation of Songhay would, in the end, cost more than it was worth: "He will have no profit out of these labours and all these expenses other than what he saves from the dues he formerly paid on merchandise. . . . This profit will be inconsiderable, and even when he raises some tribute, everything will be absorbed and more by the wages of the troops he must permanently maintain."

Some merchants who were positioned well made fortunes from the wealth. The sultan and his favorites benefited most, using the windfall to pamper themselves with luxuries. But whatever al-Mansur, his government, and the Moroccan elite may have realized from the Songhay venture, no trickle-down effect occurred. The lot of the Moroccan masses, characterized by chronic poverty, frequent famine, and periodic epidemics, remained as dismal as ever. Nor did the depredations made by the government on its own subjects decrease; even those who had money lived like paupers to hide their wealth from the sultan for fear he would confiscate it. Taxation became a game: The sultan charged his subjects fifty percent more than he intended to collect, and they were expected to cheat him out of the overcharge, giving them a sense of satisfaction. If they didn't, either because they were too intimidated, too naïve, or too honest, that was too bad for them. And if the government of Ahmad al-Mansur cost more than earlier Moroccan governments, that does not necessarily mean that his system of collecting revenue was more efficient. It may have been just more onerous.

War can never be seen as a purely economic enterprise. The Battle of Wadi al-Makhazin had unified the country and energized its people; in Moroccan terms, it was a victory of good over evil. Not so the Battle of Tondibi. Its justification as part of the holy war would need to have been followed by a real jihad, preferably the invasion and reconquest of Spain. That, of course, did not happen. If success often validates recklessness, even iniquity, the results for Ahmad al-Mansur were still mixed at best. Among those whose opinions mattered in Morocco, victory on the battlefield could never completely mask the questionable moral issues on which the enterprise had been founded.

VIII

An Ignominious Death

The successful invasion of the Songhay Empire seemed to present Ahmad al-Mansur with boundless opportunities. Morocco appeared poised to move into a new and glorious period. The Sa'di dynasty in less than a century had elbowed its way into the ranks of the great royal families, jostling with Ottomans, Hapsburgs, Bourbons, and Tudors for the spotlight. In the Western Sudan the sultan's forces, so it must have seemed, had little more to do than tie up loose ends. But loose ends stayed loose, and plundered gold was no panacea. New problems materialized, more insoluble than the old ones. The golden years for al-Dhahabi became increasingly less golden.

Changing Conditions in the South

In the Western Sudan, the Battle of Ouame at the close of 1591 proved to be the last of the Songhay army's great defeats. Now the royal family finally produced a capable leader who made a valiant effort to save what was left of Songhay. Nuh was a huge man, perhaps the largest of Dawud's legion of sons, one who had spent much of his life imprisoned by his brothers. In Nuh the Songhay had a leader equal to the Moroccan pashas, a figure who combined Mahmud's determination and Judar's flexibility. On the death of Muhammad Gao, Nuh was proclaimed Askiya of what was left of the Songhay state. Mahmud Pasha had hoped to annihilate the Songhay army at Ouame, but it seemed impossible to destroy; Nuh gave the Moroccans no further opportunities.

Songhay power was relocated to the southeast in Dendi, a moist, humid land of luxuriant vegetation noted for its stout warriors. There Askiya Nuh stopped fighting pitched battles and turned to ambush and harassment in a ferocious guerrilla war across a landscape of bush, forest, and swamplands. Here the Moroccans could not deploy their massive firepower to overwhelm their larger if ill-equipped foe. Instead they became the victims of sudden attack, losing a dozen men here, a hundred men there. In Dendi the physical environment favored the resisters rather than the invaders; the Moroccans suffered a shortage of provisions, exhaustion aggravated by climate, tropical parasites, spoiled food, and bad water. Dysentery killed more of Mahmud Pasha's men than died in battle, and malaria was at epidemic level in their camp. At one point sleeping sickness (trypanosomiasis) killed all the Moroccan horses.

Nuh enjoyed success on another front. States on the periphery of the old Songhay Empire, most of them once victims of its aggression, now came to its aid. They were a shadowy group led by Kebbi to the southeast and included some Hausa states in northern Nigeria and possibly even Morocco's erstwhile ally Bornu. Their alliance provoked al-Mansur to write one of his long epistles to the Kanta (ruler) of Kebbi, informing him that God had chosen to work "through this prophetic mission" and warning him that the Askiya had ignored a similar letter, "and you are aware of what came to pass in this affair from our vanguard, which ground him to dust." The sultan charged that in giving aid to the Songhay, Kebbi was "seeking to oppose what God had predestined for those whom He has despoiled, and for whom He has decreed perdition and woe." The kanta was instructed to stop providing support and to submit to the sultan. If "bad judgment causes you to deviate from the path," the sultan's forces would pour over the land of Kebbi, "flowing with ignominy and destruction, until—by God's might—they shall reduce your land to a barren wilderness, and bring you to the same plight as [the] Askiya, whom they made to taste death."

The angry tone of al-Mansur's letter reflects his frustration at not being able to bring the conquest to a successful conclusion.

He must have feared that the united front of resistance Kebbi represented spelled the end of his dreams to penetrate deeper into the African interior. And despite al-Mansur's threatening words, the kanta was not to be intimidated. The war continued: "Many terrible battles took place in the land," al-Sadi reports, "and Askiya Nuh and his small band were more successful against them than Askiya Ishaq had been with a force a hundred times larger." In response to Mahmud Pasha's requests, al-Mansur sent in succession six additional corps, but no amount of reinforcements could have won this war. In Dendi the Moroccan invasion ground to a halt and began to ebb. With Moroccan energy focused there, other parts of the Songhay Empire began splitting into petty states and free tribes that sometimes paid submission to the Moroccans but more often fought them. The imperial knot that had tied the Western Sudan together now lay in shreds.

In the fall of 1593 Mahmud Pasha returned to Timbuktu to take care of unfinished business. A year earlier Qadi Umar had dispatched a delegation under his nephew, Shams al-Din, to convey a letter to Ahmad al-Mansur requesting that a pardon be granted for the revolt of the previous fall and assuring the sultan that the city's ulama were now in complete obedience to him. In Marrakesh the sultan gave the delegation a warm reception and sent it back to Timbuktu with an escort supposedly carrying orders instructing Mahmud Pasha not to molest the qadi or his associates. On reaching Taghaza, the qa'id in charge confessed to Shams—to whom he had taken a liking—that other orders had gone ahead to the pasha, condemning Shams for carrying his uncle's message. Shams then escaped into Ottoman territory.

After two futile years in Dendi trying to corner Nuh, Mahmud Pasha was not in a magnanimous mood when he returned to Timbuktu. He had decided against destroying the city, which was the most convenient place for the Moroccans to maintain their headquarters. But clearly a message was in order. The pasha was also under pressure from his men, who had been frustrated by the hardships and little booty of the Dendi campaign. The uprising in Timbuktu two years earlier provided the pretext for looting the city and getting rid of its pesky ulama. In mid-October 1593, Mahmud Pasha sent around a crier announcing that various

Photo 8.1   The Sankore mosque where Mahmud Pasha ordered the arrest of the Timbuktu ulama. Courtesy of author.

sections of the Timbuktu population were to meet at different times in the Sankore mosque on the northern side of town to swear allegiance to Sultan Ahmad al-Mansur.

When the ulama's turn came, the doors of the mosque were closed and locked, and musketeers appeared. The ulama were divided into two groups and sent under armed guard to the casbah on the southern edge of town by different routes. Along the way, an altercation led to the massacre of one entire group save for a single survivor. The pasha then led his troops in a search of homes belonging to members of the clan of Qadi Umar, which included many of the city's most prominent citizens. Property was plundered, and women were stripped and raped before being imprisoned with their husbands. No estimate exists of the amount of loot taken, but al-Sadi reports what happened to it: "Mahmud Pasha wasted all the wealth he had seized and scattered it far and wide. He gave generously to his soldiers but sent nothing to Sultan Ahmad al-Mansur except 100,000 mithqals of gold."

The once proud Qadi Umar and more than seventy of his relatives and associates were sent across the Sahara to Morocco, arriving in Marrakesh on June 20, 1594. Three months later Qadi Umar died, leaving a letter addressed to Sultan al-Mansur with instructions that it be delivered after his passing. It read: "You are the oppressor and I am the one oppressed. Both oppressor and oppressed will meet before the Just Judge on the morrow." This greatly unnerved al-Mansur, who is said to have regretted his actions and to have uttered: "If I had taken anyone's advice over that decision I would wipe him out, root and branch." The decision, however, had been his alone.

As a man who believed himself something of a savant, al-Mansur may have thought that looting a famous center of learning like Timbuktu of its intelligentsia and making them part of his personal treasure added status to the position of a caliph. Once the exiles were in Marrakesh, however, the sultan seemed not to know what to do with them. Moroccan sources maintain that although the scholars were kept under house arrest, they were treated well because of the intercession of the Marrakesh ulama. Other sources claim that they suffered dismal conditions in a public prison alongside common criminals. In May 1596, the Marrakesh ulama arranged for their counterparts to be given some liberties. But the poor treatment of the Timbuktu ulama was criticized by detractors of al-Mansur within the Moroccan intellectual community for the rest of his reign, causing him considerable embarrassment.

The exiles remained a bitter and impudent lot. The most renowned was Ahmad Baba, a cousin of Qadi Umar, who was considered the premier legal scholar in the western Islamic world of his day. Shortly after the exiles were given the freedom to move about Marrakesh, Ahmad Baba went to the sultan's palace and demanded an audience. When he found al-Mansur speaking to him from behind a curtain, he was galled: "God had declared in the Qur'an," he chided, "that [only] God can address man by revelation or from behind a curtain. I see that you take God as your model, but if you wish to speak with me, come out from behind the curtain." The sultan complied, and to his face Ahmad Baba reproached him, "Why did you sack my house, steal my books, put me in chains, and bring me to

Morocco?" The sultan attempted to justify his action: "We wished to establish unity in the Muslim world and since you were one of the most distinguished representatives of Islam in your country, we expected your submission to be followed by that of your fellow citizens." Ahmad Baba replied, "If that is so, why did you not seek [first] to establish this unity amongst the Turks of Tlemcen and other places nearer to you?" The overmatched sultan soon broke off the interview.

After his release, Ahmad Baba spent his time lecturing in the main mosque in Marrakesh. Legal questions were sent for his opinion from as far away as Egypt, and he became the final arbiter of law in a city where technically he was still under house arrest. Muftis and qadis from all over Morocco came to study with him. When not lecturing or holding seminars, he found time to write; later he produced a treatise entitled *How to Obtain Blessing and Ward off Divine Wrath by Avoiding Unjust Rulers*.

Ahmad Baba and the surviving exiles had the satisfaction of knowing that one of their oppressors got his just desserts. Al-Mansur had received complaints about the cruelty and exactions imposed by Mahmud Pasha but had ignored them. Then a recently returned qa'id reported that when soldiers saluted, saying "God gives victory to the sultan," Mahmud Pasha would unsheathe his sword and reply, "Here is my sultan." This angered al-Mansur. On the arrival in Marrakesh of the caravan bringing the Timbuktu exiles, the sultan heard stories of the great wealth the pasha had looted from the homes of the ulama. Most of this, al-Mansur learned, had been squandered on the soldiers, Mahmud sending to Marrakesh what was considered a paltry sum. The pasha could have had only one reason for doing this: by being more generous with his troops than with his master, he was trying to secure his own position in the conquered territory. The sultan ordered another pasha, Mansur b. Abd al-Rahman, to go to the Western Sudan, arrest Mahmud, and inflict an "ignominious death" on him. When Abu Faris, one of the sultan's sons and a longtime patron of Mahmud, heard this, he sent his own messenger to warn the pasha.

Abu Faris's warning reached Mahmud in January 1595 as he was fighting in a mountainous area against a unit of Nuh's partisans, who had taken positions atop a rocky precipice. The pasha did not fear death, only an ignominious one. That night he took fifty men on a suicide mission to scale the cliffs. In the resulting encounter he was killed and his head sent to Nuh, who passed it on to Kebbi, where it was displayed in the marketplace at the capital.

Changing Conditions in the North

When Mahmud Pasha died, the Moroccans had been in the Western Sudan for almost four years. During that period al-Mansur's focus may have been too strongly fixed on his project on the other side of the Sahara. His grip on Morocco had started to slip, beginning with a rapid slide in his popularity. To those who mattered, he had told too many lies. For the majority who, in a sultan's mind, probably did not matter and who wanted little more than to be left alone, his demands made their lives increasingly miserable. His war on the Songhay Empire had brought little relief.

To outside observers, Sultan Ahmad al-Mansur was still in control: "The Xeriffo is absolute Lord of all his subjects' goods, yea and of their persons also. For though he charge them with ever so burdensome tributes, and impositions; yet dare they not so much as open their mouths." This was the observation of John Pory, who may have underestimated the degree of resentment. Increasingly the sultan's behavior was seen as being beyond the bounds for one whose claims made him the exemplar for all Muslims.

António de Saldanha tells of an Andalusian merchant named Monfadal, who had served al-Mansur well but who had a daughter of "extraordinary beauty." Monfadal adored her and allowed her considerable freedom, for example, to dress in the manner she pleased and to read books in Spanish about chivalry. Unfortunately, she caught the sultan's eye, and "being the sensual Moor that he was," he desired to have her. Monfadal "knew the custom of the Moors of making their women slaves" and did not want her languishing in a harem for the rest of her life. He managed to put off the sultan's advances for a while, but "his desires did not stop growing." The sultan finally warned Monfadal, then sent a qa'id to seize her. Monfadal went into a swoon and died within six hours. The grief-stricken daughter followed him two months later. António de Saldanha called it "a tragedy without doubt unique in the memory of men." Sultans, like kings everywhere, were expected to symbolize the virility of their people—but within prescribed limits: Freeborn Muslim men and women were not to be treated as chattel.

In 1595 Sultan Ahmad al-Mansur was put on notice that all was not well in the state of Morocco. Mercenaries led by al-Nasir b. al-Ghalib, a brother of al-Mutawakkil, invaded Morocco from a Spanish enclave on the Mediterranean coast. Although the Spanish denied culpability, there was no doubt that al-Nasir was their man. Al-Nasir had fought on the side of al-Mutawakkil at Wadi al-Makhazin and had been one of the few to escape the carnage, eventually ending up in Madrid. Al-Mansur had requested several times that al-Nasir be turned over to Moroccan authorities, but the Spanish had refused. A pretender to someone else's throne was a valuable asset, and apparently Philip thought the time had come to use it.

Al-Mansur's well developed spy network kept him apprised of al-Nasir's expedition from the time it materialized in Spain, and Moroccan forces led by Crown Prince al-Shaykh al-Ma'mun were ready in the north. A pretender associated with a discredited cause who was supported by the Spanish should not have had much chance to gain support in Morocco. Al-Mansur referred to al-Nasir's followers as "the polytheists and friends of the party of Satan, the renegade unbelievers." Yet as al-Nasir marched toward Fez, he was joined by an alarming number of Berber tribesmen, and reportedly there was sympathy for his cause as far away as the Sus. In the end, however, al-Nasir was no match for the military abilities of the crown prince or, according to António de Saldanha, for al-Ma'mun's chief general, a renegade named Mustafa Pasha, who defeated the invaders in two battles, in August 1595 and May 1596. Following the second, al-Shaykh al-Ma'mun sent his cousin's head back to Marrakesh.

It was no accident that al-Nasir's initial objective was Fez, which he may have hoped would rise in his support. After al-Nasir's defeat, al-Mansur thanked the leaders of Fez for their love of his dynasty and their "courageous opposition to the party of Satan." But Crown Prince al-Shaykh al-Ma'mun, who ruled there as viceroy, was not popular in the city. Fear rather than love had probably kept the Fezi in line, at least until the battlefield determined which side would prevail. The al-Nasir affair should have been a warning to the man in power, yet there is no indication of a change in either policy or behavior, and no attempt was made to address the issues that had made the revolt a real threat, the first to al-Mansur since the early years of his reign.

Unleashing al-Nasir against al-Mansur was not one of King Philip II's more judicious foreign policy decisions. While publicly professing their animosity toward each other, Spain and Morocco had enjoyed years of détente bordering at times on alliance against the Ottoman Empire. In the same year that al-Nasir invaded Morocco, Spain became involved in an open war with France, putting that country on an enemies list that already included England and the Dutch Republic. It seemed no time to add Morocco as well. Al-Fishtali claims that Philip feared the growing power of Morocco: "He perceived the greatness of the Islamic, lordly Mansuri government, the large number of people, important people, delegated to reorganize the navy and to increase the number of jihad war ships, and the amount of war equipment." Philip was said to be concerned that al-Mansur was planning an invasion of Spain: "Our lord, the Commander of the Faithful (may God support him) wanted to cross the sea with the Divine forces and the soldiers of Islam with which he wanted to conquer al-Andalus and take it away from the hands of the unbelievers."

Spain had indeed become a problem for al-Mansur. He had promised his ulama that the conquest of the Songhay Empire would help to unify Islam, allowing him to turn against the infidel and reconquer the Iberian peninsula. In the real world of geopolitics, the loot of the Western Sudan did not make Morocco strong enough to challenge Spain without an alliance with the Ottoman Empire, and the Moroccans knew that if Spain were defeated, the Ottomans would fill the resulting vacuum. But al-Mansur was stuck with his promise. Instead of deeds he used words, threatening to invade Spain. Spanish complicity in the al-Nasir affair seemed to goad al-Mansur into retaliating. He was furious with Philip, and al-Zayyani believes that at this time the sultan made up his mind to attack Spain and would have, once preparations were completed, had not unforseeable circumstances intervened. Many letters to noted holy men as far off as Mecca asked for their prayers in what al-Mansur indicated was the imminent reconquest of Andalusia. However, no military action was forthcoming.

Al-Fishtali, it turns out, was right—up to a point. Al-Mansur's jihadist propaganda, designed to gain support from fellow Muslims for his claim to the caliphate, was so effective it convinced Philip II that Morocco had become a real threat. The Spanish were probably aware of popular discontent in Morocco and had hoped that al-Nasir's invasion would at least generate trouble. With some luck, Morocco would plunge into civil war, immobilizing any danger to Spain, and with more luck, Morocco might come apart, allowing Philip the opportunity to eradicate the pirate nests that lay along the Moroccan coast. But the Spanish had no more intention of invading Morocco than the Moroccans had of invading Spain. For Spain, as long as the truce with the Ottoman Empire held, Morocco was increasingly relegated to a sideshow.

Ever able to capitalize on the missteps of others, al-Mansur used Spain's role in the al-Nasir invasion to divert public attention from an unhappy domestic scene. All Morocco was mobilized to rally around the Sa'di dynasty, which again assumed the role of saviors of the country from foreign invaders. The Spanish had been useful when the Ottomans were a problem, but by the end of the sixteenth century the Turkish threat was rapidly receding. Good relations with Madrid could be sacrificed so long as the rulers of both Morocco and Spain had no intention of going to war. The safest way to keep Spain off guard was to draw closer to its European enemies. The most bitter and determined enemy of Spain was now the Dutch Republic, but the Sa'dis had always preferred to deal with the English, whom they felt they knew better. Once again al-Mansur turned to a now aging Queen Elizabeth.

As far as the English were concerned, Morocco had been an enemy of their enemy, which sometimes meant a friend if never quite an ally-in-arms, and the two had been commercial partners. However, al-Mansur's unreliable conduct in the Dom António matter lingered among English foreign policy makers. Despite professions of friendship on both sides and flowery words from the sultan in praise of the queen, relations in the 1590s never regained the level they had enjoyed in the 1580s. Much of the correspondence between the two monarchs now involved the plight of English merchants who were trying to do business in Morocco and found themselves languishing in Moroccan prisons.

On a broader level, the winds of international politics were beginning to shift, and the long English struggle against Spain was winding down. Al-Mansur must have sensed a standoffishness on the part of the English, and in 1600 he sent an ambassador to London, empowered to make a deal committing the two states to a joint attack on Spain. The English were skeptical. A rumor spread that the mission's real intent was to conduct commercial espionage. In fact, the Moroccans did take considerable interest in technological advances, mechanical devices, and astronomical instruments, reflecting al-Mansur's own curiosity. If English suspicions in this matter appear overblown, they reflected the general English attitude toward al-Mansur at the time.

In the negotiations that followed, al-Mansur's representatives offered grain to England even though a famine was raging in Morocco. They also offered to man English warships with Moroccan sailors even though the Moroccan navy was minuscule by English standards. The English were not impressed; they suspected the Moroccans of trying to manipulate them into attacking Spain in order to relieve pressure on Morocco. However, Elizabeth could not afford to insult al-Mansur openly, so she proposed that the discussions be continued in Marrakesh. To conduct them, she sent a low-level emissary, a common merchant, who proposed that al-Mansur give Elizabeth £100,000 in gold to rebuild the English fleet. Al-Mansur agreed in return for an offensive alliance in which a joint Anglo-Moroccan fleet would conquer the Spanish colonial empire. In this, his wildest proposal yet, the Spanish colonies would be divided according to climate, with the hot lands, specifically the West Indies, going to Morocco and the temperate lands to England. The image of Muslim states scattered across an Islamic Caribbean led by the true caliph was an extraordinary one, just the challenge Ahmad al-Mansur would judge himself capable of handling. To press the matter, al-Mansur wrote to Elizabeth, assuring her that the Muslim inhabitants of the Caribbean islands would welcome an Anglo-Moroccan invasion. Not surprisingly, negotiations stalled. While Elizabeth's government may have considered the Moroccans untrustworthy, the English themselves did not always take the high road in their dealings, as in 1603 when the English ambassador to Marrakesh wrote his royal sovereign to encourage consideration of an English invasion of Morocco.

If al-Mansur could afford to be more arbitrary in his dealings with the Spanish, it was because relations between Morocco and the Ottoman Empire were also changing. The Ottomans had concluded that Morocco was too far from the center of Turkish gravity to bother with and that adding another semi-desert territory to their holdings probably wasn't worth the effort. The Ottoman Empire had too many frontiers, and North Africa was steadily slipping downward on its priority list. Even the usually aggressive garrison next door in Algiers had become preoccupied with internal matters and no longer looked for excuses to march on Fez. On the surface it appeared that Algiers and Marrakesh were entering a period of détente. During the al-Nasir revolt the Turks in Algiers had provided some intelligence, which was welcomed, and offered military support, which was declined. Al-Mansur likewise offered assistance to the authorities in Algiers when rebellion flared among the Berbers of the Kabylia Mountains. He railed indignantly at the rebel leader for seeking aid from the unbelieving Spanish. Nevertheless, there is suspicion that al-Mansur first aided and encouraged the rebels, then covered his tracks by offering to help subdue them.

Qadi Umar's Curse

Al-Mansur's success against the Songhay Empire did not alter his relations with his neighbors. If the showy displays of wealth impressed them, this did not allow Morocco to rise even a notch in the power scheme that had characterized the Mediterranean geopolitical world since his accession. The armies that now should have marched north and east to create the caliphate remained bogged down in West Africa.

Mahmud Pasha's successor, Mansur b. Abd al-Rahman, arrived in Timbuktu in March 1595. Shortly thereafter he rallied the troops to seek revenge for Mahmud Pasha's death (even if he had been sent originally with the purpose of bringing that about), and in the battle that followed the Moroccans inflicted on Askiya Nuh the greatest defeat of his career. However, when Mansur Pasha tried to remove Judar from his command, the power struggle that ensued ended with the sudden death of Mansur Pasha. According to rumor, Judar poisoned him. The sultan replaced Mansur Pasha with Muhammad Taba, who took control in 1597. He had been one of Sultan Abd al-Malik's top generals who somehow escaped execution when al-Mansur purged the military but had spent most of the intervening years in prison. Within five months, Muhammad Taba also died of a bellyful of poison.

The sultan bowed to the inevitable and quit sending pashas for Judar to kill. In March 1599, al-Mansur recalled Judar to Marrakesh, not to answer for crimes against his fellow officers but to help put down a new rebellion. Judar had no personal ambition beyond running the conquered territories for his master; his plotting and murdering were done with the conviction that he was doing the best for the sultan, and al-Mansur seems to have accepted this. Judar went home for a promotion and never returned. In the year Judar left, Askiya Nuh was overthrown. His defeat by Mansur Pasha had undermined his position just enough to make him vulnerable to the court intrigue that still plagued Songhay. The remnant of the royal family replaced him with another brother, and within a few years several more brothers were also elevated and deposed. Fortunately for the Songhay, the Moroccan offense had sputtered to a halt, no longer powered by Judar and Mahmud Pasha, men who were brave, efficient, and cruel in the name of a master who gave them power to destroy but not to rebuild. Throughout this period, the presence of Sultan Ahmad al-Mansur hovered like some malevolent cloud that periodically sent bolts to shatter the Songhay. Eventually al-Mansur ran out of bolts.

The longest-lived of the major characters in the post-Tondibi drama enjoyed the happiest ending. One of al-Mansur's sons, Zaydan, a great admirer of Ahmad Baba, once promised that he would free the scholar if he ever had the opportunity. Zaydan did come to power, and in 1607 Ahmad Baba held him to his word. The great scholar returned to Timbuktu, where he spent the last twenty years of his life teaching and writing, the only one of the exiles who saw his homeland again. Years earlier, in 1594, when the exiles from Timbuktu first reached Marrakesh, Qadi Umar had cursed the Sa'dis: "Oh my God!" he wailed, "They have tormented us and have made us leave our country; torment them and make it so that they must leave their country." When it was uttered, Qadi Umar's curse seemed to echo in a void. But in the years that followed, Morocco suffered a host of problems, including famine, plague, and increasing lawlessness, that the government seemed unable to resolve. Worse, the dynasty itself began splitting apart.

After the Songhay invasion, al-Mansur increasingly withdrew into the confines of the Badi. Family issues, about which the outside world heard only occasional rumblings, preoccupied much of his time. His mother died in the year after Tondibi, and his sons, supported by their mothers, became more blatant in advancing their own agendas. His third son, Abu al-Hasan, who had shown himself to be the most capable of the royal brothers, was assassinated in 1593 by a Spaniard who harbored a personal grudge. As al-Mansur became more and more distracted by private matters, António de Saldanha notes, "he gave the country over to the soldiers." Problems were especially evident in the north, where the sultan's presence might have had a settling effect. But court astrologers began warning al-Mansur that if he ever crossed the Sebu River, which flowed south of Fez, he would never return to Marrakesh. For the time being, the north would just have to stay troubled.

Al-Mansur was said to have had a dozen sons, whom he appointed governors of different regions, with Muhammad al-Shaykh al-Ma'mun serving as viceroy at Fez. Following a serious illness early in his reign, al-Mansur proclaimed al-Ma'mun his successor in 1581 and, in case any doubt lingered, again in 1585. At both times, notables—ulama, tribal leaders, military commanders, and the sultan's extended family, including his younger sons—attended and were required to take an oath to the heir designate. The second ceremony was a spectacular affair. Father and son approached each other, leading their respective armies, until at a certain point al-Ma'mun dismounted and kissed al-Mansur on the foot. The sultan then nodded, and al-Ma'mun remounted, after which the two rode off together to where a magnificent tent had been erected. Al-Fishtali had drawn up a long formal document for the notables to swear to, in which he traced the history of the caliphate down to al-Mansur. This turned out to be as much a celebration of the glory of al-Mansur as an affirmation of his successor. On the conclusion of the ceremony, poems were read and the sultan distributed gifts.

Described as having "a deep red-brick complexion, protruding eyes, a pronounced nose, thick lips and a piercing voice," al-Ma'mun proved himself gifted as a military commander, a markedly better one than any of his brothers and all but the best of his father's generals. And he was brave. At a critical point in the battle that ended al-Nasir's rebellion, al-Ma'mun is said to have taken a position in the middle of his frontline troops, rallying them with an arquebus in one hand and a ball of lead tucked into his cheek. Al-Fishtali praises al-Ma'mun as a ruler with many good qualities, but al-Fishtali is really praising al-Mansur's personnel decision in selecting this son as his heir. The antics of the crown prince, however, would begin the subversion that would bring the dynasty to ruin.

If al-Shaykh al-Ma'mun was an effective soldier, he was a bad ruler. In Fez he used the considerable latitude his father gave him to oppress his subjects, whether loyal or rebellious, high or low. He allowed his army to get out of control, "appropriating cattle and carpets, debauching the women of the country [and] renting out the casbah each day for a price in gold," apparently for purposes of prostitution and other illicit activities, according to al-Ifrani. The crown prince behaved even worse than his soldiers. He plundered his own tax collectors, then declared that all the funds they had collected were null and void, and new tax collectors were sent out to collect the full amount again: "The result was that most of the laborers stopped farming and that, for those who continued, the officials imposed double what should have been, such that they [the people] had nothing left." And if al-Shaykh al-Ma'mun's public behavior was insufferable, his private doings were repugnant: "Debauched, of ignoble character," al-Ifrani writes, "al-Ma'mun was passionate about unnatural love and gave himself over to drink; besides he was bloodthirsty and indifferent to all matters of religion, prayers or other practices." António de Saldanha admits there was a problem but portrays al-Ma'mun less as a rogue devoted to evildoing by his base nature than as an incompetent who was drunk from too much wine most of the time.

Al-Mansur had a difficult time accepting the enormity of his son's shortcomings. He blamed part of the problem on al-Ma'mun's entourage, "his companions in debauchery, who surrounded him in a crowd, drawing fire from his wickedness and encouraging him in his resistance and his rebellion." The sultan hoped that al-Ma'mun's conscience would "return him to the good path and cause to be born in him the desire to tear himself away from his misdeeds or at least curb them." But al-Mansur's hopes were in vain: Al-Shaykh al-Ma'mun had no conscience, and he was impervious to advice from steadier quarters. When one of his father's viziers tried to talk to him about his "odious conduct," al-Ma'mun poisoned him: "Finally, his exactions becoming more numerous, and [with] complaints arriving from all sides, the sultan wrote to his son to cease his excesses and to end his misconduct and his abuse of power. But all these reproaches only excited al-Ma'mun." The crown prince began to carry on his own foreign policy. While al-Mansur was moving away from the Spanish, al-Ma'mun was edging toward them. His machinations provoked the Turks to the brink of a war that was prevented only by a humiliating apology from al-Mansur.

Although al-Shaykh al-Ma'mun's conduct became increasingly outrageous and the chorus of his critics steadily rose, the sultan held out against the obvious solution. Anyone else would have been put to an ignominious death, but al-Mansur had a soft spot for this son: "His desire to see him come to power was so strong," according to al-Ifrani, "that he never affixed his seal on the smallest sack of money of the treasury without saying: 'May God make this seal replaced by the hand of al-Shaykh!'" Another son, Zaydan, who sought to displace al-Ma'mun, took advantage of the situation by convincing his father to order the death of al-Ma'mun's second-in-command, Mustafa Pasha, whose head was dutifully delivered to Marrakesh. Actually Mustafa had been a positive influence who had kept Fez from completely collapsing into anarchy. Matters there got worse. Even the normally pliant viziers and military commanders now recommended that the prince be eliminated for the good of the country: "'None of you suggest anything to me about the death of my son,' al-Mansur roared at one pasha. 'Great God,' replied [Pasha] Aziz, 'I have given you the most profitable advice, and when the day of the Resurrection will come, I will be in the truth before God as I am before you and these people.'"

If the crown prince was not to be executed, al-Mansur realized he would have to be neutralized. Despite continued warnings not to cross the Sebu, in October 1602, al-Mansur took an army of twelve thousand on a forced march north and surrounded Fez. The crown prince managed to escape with his retinue and part of his army. Al-Mansur then sent Judar Pasha in pursuit, resulting in a brutal three-hour battle in which the sultan's side prevailed and the crown prince was captured. He was sent to Meknes, thirty miles west of Fez, and thrown into prison while his father pondered what to do with him. Al-Mansur considered this war and his son's imprisonment a catastrophe, and he appeared never to recover from it. Although al-Ma'mun remained in prison for the rest of his father's life, the sultan never stripped him of his designation as crown prince. On matters of succession al-Mansur seemed paralyzed. The consequences for his dynasty and the country would be disastrous.

The fall of al-Ma'mun brought two other brothers to the fore. Abu Faris Abd Allah al-Wathiq, the second oldest and a full brother of al-Ma'mun, is described by al-Ifrani as "a pot-bellied man, a big eater [who was] subject to attacks of epilepsy." António de Saldanha characterizes him as "not very capable" and implies that unlike his brothers he was something of a coward, "not a man to go out on campaign and risk his own safety." Abu Faris became the sultan's lieutenant in Marrakesh while Zaydan al-Nasir, the fourth son, who had played a significant role in the campaign to bring al-Ma'mun to heel, was made governor of Fez. This appointment should have been accompanied by an acknowledgment that he was now crown prince, but it wasn't. Zaydan is described as having "a yellowish complexion" and as being "brave, audacious and having taken part personally in combats." Zaydan's mother was a noblewoman, unlike the mother of al-Ma'mun and Abu Faris, who was a concubine albeit a forceful woman who did not hesitate to play a role when given the opportunity. To al-Ifrani, Zaydan was hardly a hero, but he comes across as the best of a bad lot. To António de Saldanha, Zaydan was a schemer and a rascal bent on undermining his older brother at whatever the cost to his father and the country.

For whatever reason, al-Mansur was not to be swayed by arguments in favor of Zaydan, and, according to António de Saldanha, the sultan was quite annoyed with him for causing so much trouble. Al-Ma'mun's mother convinced a group of notables from Marrakesh to beseech the sultan on behalf of her son, and al-Mansur allowed them to go to Meknes and interview him: "When the notables found themselves in the presence of al-Shaykh, they were amazed that he was more perverse than ever and they were even witness to things so ignoble on his part, that language cannot describe them." This according to al-Ifrani, whose loathing of al-Ma'mun looms large in his work. However perverse and ignoble the prince may have been before the delegation, it returned to the sultan with the report that al-Ma'mun had changed for the better. But one of the notables could not stand the charade and confessed that he could not lie before God; he told the sultan that his son was "always motivated by his perverse instincts; his feelings are evil, his intentions culpable; he does not express the least remorse about what has happened, and he has renounced neither his turpitudes nor his outbreaks." Al-Shaykh al-Ma'mun stayed in prison.

António de Saldanha does not mention the visit by the notables; on the contrary, in his account al-Ma'mun's mother died shortly before al-Mansur marched against her son. But he does report on a secret meeting in which al-Ma'mun was brought from Meknes to see his father, who was camped outside Fez. Al-Mansur greeted his son with a hug and led him to a great feast that they enjoyed together with the sultan's qa'ids. Afterward, the father and son retired into a tent where only a sister of al-Ma'mun was present. At the end of the interview, al-Mansur rejoined his qa'ids, to whom he announced that "his son was good for nothing." Al-Ma'mun was returned to prison.

Two short but bloody internal wars, a steady elevation in the level of civil unrest due to heavy government exactions, and the depraved ways of the crown prince signaling moral corruption at the highest level were interpreted by many Moroccans as further signs of the millennial convulsions that would lead to the end of the world. In the last decades of the sixteenth century calamities began to pile up. A famine in 1577 came to be known as the Years of Grass after the diet common to many people. The suffering reached its peak in 1579–1580, when a deadly influenza carried many away. The time was ripe for the coming of the Mahdi, but in the years following the conquest of the Western Sudan, al-Mansur's record was unconvincing. He did not seem to be the solution to the problems; indeed, the calamities were happening to him and to those he was supposed to protect.

Of all the calamities, epidemic disease was the most terrifying because it was the least understood. Identifying specific diseases from the past is very difficult because in most cases the descriptions of symptoms are vague at best. The most virulent scourge was bubonic plague, which is always suspected when plague is mentioned, but the tendency has been to attribute every epidemic of that era to this one malady. In North Africa all epidemics were generally referred to by the vague term "waba," while in West Africa observers did just the opposite, giving each individual epidemic a separate name. Epidemics had struck Morocco in 1521–1522, 1557–1558, and 1580. In 1596 a pandemic swept northern Spain, killing an estimated ten percent of that country's population. Modern speculation for this outbreak has focused on cholera, but this is problematic. Cholera is endemic to India, where it seems to have remained until the late eighteenth century; it does not appear in Europe until the 1830s. Reports of bubonic plague in North Africa, however, go back to the third century B.C.E., and an especially disastrous case had almost caused the economy to collapse in the 1350s.

Whatever the diagnosis of the disease that appeared in 1596, it was extraordinarily virulent. A year later it jumped to Morocco, showing up in Fez in February 1597. In the spring of the following year it spread throughout the country, killing at its height a thousand people a day in Fez and two thousand a day in Marrakesh. According to a Spanish source, an estimated 450,000 succumbed across North Africa. On June 24, 1599, Queen Elizabeth wrote to Sultan al-Mansur to express concern "for the preservation of your health, so precious."

Al-Mansur dealt with the catastrophe by "taking to the tents," that is, camping outside the cities as much as possible. When he traveled in this manner, the sultan hardly lived the rough life. His domicile was a virtual portable court with connected tents, pavilions, and canopies supported by wooden frames and walls complete with doors, domes, and a throne room. Taking to the tents may have been a viable strategy for escaping the plague, but for al-Mansur it meant traveling with his army, and army camps were probably the one setting more susceptible to the spread of disease than cities. The plague swept through his army, killing so many of his trusted troops that he had to recruit Christian slaves to reinforce his own bodyguard. One cavalry unit of 3,000 was reported to have been wiped out to the last man. With the army neutralized and the state nearly paralyzed, revolts broke out in many places. The Sus sugar mills were vandalized by resentful peasants who had been exploited by the industry in better times, causing considerable damage to the export economy.

The fury of the plague abated between 1599 and 1601. But it hid out in the south, apparently among people whose deaths went unnoticed, then reappeared with a vengeance to a population now weakened by drought. In the spring of 1602 it was raging in the Sus; eventually it would kill an estimated one-third to one-half of the entire country's inhabitants. Al-Mansur was getting ready to return from Fez, having put down al-Ma'mun's insurrection when reports of the disaster began to pour in.

In August 1603 the sultan camped at Zahr al-Zawuia, a short distance from Fez on the road to Marrakesh. It was the time of the 'Id al-Mawlid, the celebration of the Prophet's birthday. Although he had not visited Fez for many years, al-Mansur could not resist being in the middle of a great city on this particular holiday. While there he became so tired he had to be carried back to camp. He called his qa'ids to his bedside and ordered them to recognize Abu Faris as ruler of Marrakesh and Zaydan as ruler of Fez. Their older brother, al-Shaykh al-Ma'mun, was to be delivered to Abu Faris. The sultan commanded that all three live in peace and friendship.

Within a short time, Ahmad al-Mansur developed symptoms, according to al-Ifrani, although he does not describe what they

Photo 8.2 The Sa'dian tombs in Marrakesh. Courtesy of author.

were. For the bubonic form of plague, they would include a blackish rash followed by swollen lymph nodes in the groin and under the armpits—the buboes—accompanied by fever and eventually delirium. Cholera would start with violent spasms of vomiting and diarrhea, causing dehydration so severe the victim's blood would coagulate and the skin would appear to turn blue. For both diseases, death generally came within five days. Indeed al-Mansur took to bed, where he languished for five miserable days. All the gold in the mythical Wangara could not save him from his own ignominious death, which occurred on August 20. His body was carried to Marrakesh and interred in the Sa'dian tombs, among his family.

IX

Postmortem

Ahmad al-Mansur was the last of the great Sa'di sultans. The dynasty had remained in power and kept the country together largely because of the particular abilities of each ruler. Morocco was divided in many ways: into great cities, bountiful plains, and huge expanses of waste; burning sands, cloud-shrouded forests, and snowcapped mountains; Arab nomads, Berber farmers, and Andalusian exiles; men of the book, men of the sword, and men of the souk. The Sa'di government had to stretch itself across different peoples, different economies, and different landscapes. Sa'di despotism had to find a balance between being too oppressive and too lax; either one would have brought the dynasty down. So would have mediocre leadership. Just as the Sa'di state had been created by strong men, other strong men would have to keep it together until its institutions became firmly established. At the time of al-Mansur's death this had not happened; the Moroccan state was still a frail assemblage. After him, as the Anonymous Chronicler of Fez remarks, "all of the bad people who had remained away came back and all of the good people who had been in evidence beat a retreat."

Al-Ifrani warns his readers against an alternative and, he believes, spurious account of al-Mansur's death: "A popular legend reports that al-Mansur was poisoned by his son Zaydan at the instigation of his mother by means of a fig that Zaydan offered his father." At the point of death, al-Mansur told his son: "You are too much in a hurry, oh Zaydan; may it please God never to let you enjoy power peacefully." This alternative account appears as fact in the Anonymous Chronicler of Fez, but al-Ifrani is certain that the plague was responsible, and today his account is almost universally accepted. As long as al-Mansur lived, Zaydan could hope that his father would come to his senses and fix the succession. Now the abyss awaited.

Warring Brothers

The immediate consequence of al-Mansur's death was to throw Morocco into confusion. Zaydan was in Fez, Abu Faris was in Marrakesh, and al-Shaykh al-Ma'mun was still in prison in Meknes. Each thought himself the rightful heir, and each had some support. Zaydan and Abu Faris were both proclaimed sultan, and both claimed to be caliph. Soon they were at war with each other. Al-Ma'mun was later freed by Abu Faris and put in command of an army with orders to drive Zaydan from Fez. This he did, and he celebrated by proclaiming himself sultan.

Thus began a three-way fratricidal war that would last a decade, leaving the dynasty and the country in shreds. Through the twists and turns of a wildly complicated series of conflicts, the rival claimants sometimes switched cities. Al-Ma'mun had the assistance of his murderous son, Abd Allah, and they were generally successful on the battlefield. But their rule proved so obnoxious to the civilian population that they and their soldiers were often chased out of one city or another by enraged townspeople. This gave Zaydan, who time and again appeared almost incapable of winning a battle, the opportunity to reoccupy whatever city his enemies did not then control. Battles were bloody, and the casualties for a single encounter were often reported to be in the thousands. Massacres became commonplace, including those of soldiers who had surrendered on the promise of safe conduct. In the winter of 1607–1608, after Abd Allah had occupied Marrakesh and ordered the execution of all government officials, conditions became so bad that a large part of the population abandoned the city and moved into the nearby mountains.

By 1609 Morocco was locked in its own self-inflicted death throes. The word "catastrophe" understates what the combination of civil war, plague, and famine wrought. The plague had not gone away; it continued to rage until 1610, joined between 1604 and 1608 by a famine brought on by drought. In the final year of the famine, children disappeared from city streets, the victims of adult hunger. The Dutch representative in Marrakesh reported to his government: "All is ruined, all is lost in the misery of their time, and it is impossible for me to describe what I have seen and how I have lived here."

Misfortune would catch up to most of those responsible for this tragedy, but not before the damage was irreversible. The first of the major players to be dispatched was Judar Pasha, an Abu Faris supporter, who fell into the clutches of Abd Allah in December 1606 and was put to death. Indeed, virtually all the experienced officers who had served the Sa'di state since Wadi al-Makhazin and had not been sent to the Western Sudan died in support of one brother or another during this time. In 1609, Abd Allah and Abu Faris reconciled to defeat Zaydan. Shortly thereafter Abd Allah had Abu Faris strangled as he sat on his prayer rug in his bedroom, surrounded by his wives. In the meantime al-Ma'mun sought the help of the Spanish, which he bought for the price of Larache. But in giving away the old port that had been the object of so much contention, al-Shaykh al-Ma'mun finally crossed the line. His actions, according to al-Ifrani, "produced violent feelings of anger in the hearts of the Muslims and excited a universal reprobation." On September 11, 1613, a group of local shaykhs infiltrated his camp, assassinated him, and killed a number of his followers and children. This left two Sa'di claimants still in the field. Zaydan and Abd Allah could have had a final showdown to determine who would reign supreme, unify the country, and save the dynasty; instead their armies settled into a standoff, with Zaydan in Marrakesh and Abd Allah in Fez.

Al-Mansur's failure to establish a workable succession ensured the death of his dynasty. The Sa'dis had come to power under the banner of national unity, but after 1603 they did their best to subvert it. Within a decade the country was split into two states, a north and a south, soon to be joined by an east and a west.

The Apocalypse Comes to the Western Sudan

As Morocco slipped into chaos, few people north of the Dar'a Valley paid much attention to the Western Sudan. In 1612 a qa'id named Ali b. Abd Allah al-Tilimsani deposed and murdered the pasha, an Abu Faris appointee, and declared himself pasha. Five years later al-Tilimsani was overthrown by his own soldiers, who wrote to Zaydan informing him of their action and elected one of their own as a replacement. The letter prompted Zaydan to look into the matter, and in March 1618 he sent a representative, Ammar Pasha, to Timbuktu to assess the situation. Ammar spent three months before returning to Marrakesh. The army, he told the sultan, was in a state of permanent mutiny, and the political system had deteriorated beyond repair. Twenty-eight years after Judar marched to Tondibi, the Moroccan government decided unofficially to abandon its Sudanese enterprise.

Henceforth the conquered portions of the Western Sudan remained in theory a part of the Moroccan Empire as long as Morocco was under Sa'di rule. The Friday prayer was said in the sultan's name, and the government in Timbuktu received official confirmation from the sultan whenever a new pasha was elected by the soldiers. But the pashas were in fact independent sovereigns. They named their own ministers and surrounded themselves with minuscule courts. Their state became known as the pashalik, a form of government somewhat awkwardly characterized as a military republic. Technically, the pasha was a military governor-general, but in practice he was an elected kinglet.

The Moroccan conquerors of the Western Sudan not only founded a new state, their descendants eventually constituted a new ethnic group. From the outset women had been among the spoils of war, and when the soldiers realized they were not going home, they took wives from respectable Songhay families. The children of these unions intermarried, producing a people who became known as the Arma (from the Arabic "al-rumat," literally "shooter"). In 1646 soldiers elected the first pasha who had been born in the Western Sudan, al-Tilimsani's son, Ahmad. He lasted thirteen weeks, but his elevation signaled that the native Arma had come of age. In 1659–1660 the imam in Timbuktu began saying the Friday prayer in the pasha's name, officially recognizing him as the ultimate political authority in Islam as far as the local ulama were concerned. Henceforth, in name as well as in fact, the Pasha of Timbuktu, not the Sultan of Morocco, ruled the lands of the Western Sudan.

For a people bred in the hierarchical traditions of the military, the Arma were exceedingly fractious. They fought among themselves, garrison versus garrison, division versus division, family versus family. These internecine conflicts were mostly insignificant power struggles or vendettas intended to settle the many real and imagined affronts the Arma exchanged with each other. A warrior people who expect to dominate others cannot afford the luxury of fighting among themselves, yet the Arma reveled in it. As they turned their energies inward, their control over others slipped away.

The Moroccans had won the war against Songhay because of their firepower and superior discipline, but neither survived very long into the Arma period. As ties with Morocco faded, so did access to modern weaponry; the Arma became armed with antiques. One of the more warlike groups that became a problem for the Arma was the Tuaregs. By the end of the century, the Tuaregs had come to realize that a determined cavalry charge could reach the ranks of the musketeers if the attackers were prepared to suffer casualties, usually from two volleys. This was shown in spectacular fashion on May 23, 1737, at the Battle of Toya when a charge of Tuaregs smashed into the assembled ranks of Arma, killing the pasha and half of his army. Another disastrous war against the Tuaregs in 1770–1771 finished the Arma as an effective fighting force.

The pashalik proved to be an extraordinarily unstable system of government. Between 1671 and 1750 it changed hands 114 times, with reigns averaging eleven months in the second half of the seventeenth century and eight months in the eighteenth. Pashas ruled for months, weeks, or days. One was elected and deposed on the same day in 1697. Sixteen pashas were installed more than once; one managed to be elected and deposed seven times, which was quite an achievement considering that an alarming number of pashas were assassinated or executed on their dethronement. In the eighteenth century there were long periods of interregnum during which no pasha was elected and no one ruled; the pasha had become irrelevant to the pashalik. In 1794 two pashas were elected to power in succession, both serving for just under a year. Thereafter the record of who ruled becomes so obscure as to be indecipherable. This was no way to run a government, if indeed by the end of the eighteenth century the pashalik could be considered as such.

Political instability was not the worst of West Africa's problems. Even as al-Mansur dreamed of unlimited wealth, long-term economic processes were undermining the trans-Saharan gold trade. A large part of the Akan gold production was being diverted to European trading posts on the Gulf of Guinea. Far more important, West Africa's time as a major producer of gold had entered its twilight phase. Beginning in the late sixteenth century, American gold and silver poured into Europe and then spread around the world. West Africa could not compete, and the West African gold trade petered out. When Africa reemerged as the world's premier producer of gold in the late nineteenth century, the mines were located four thousand miles away, in the Transvaal of South Africa.

The decline of the gold trade reflected an overall economic downturn impacted by a series of natural catastrophes. Beginning in 1639, frequent disasters occurred in a pattern that became the standard for two centuries: The price of food became excessive, people died of starvation, the dead were left unburied, many of the hungry ate the cadavers, and disease decimated the survivors. The crisis of 1639 began with a famine followed by a great flood. Conditions were so bad, according to al-Sadi, "that women ate their own children." Between 1657 and 1660 bubonic plague struck, followed a decade later by a drought that wiped out the harvest of 1670. Epidemics reappeared in 1672, 1688, and 1695. The last of them raged on and off until 1704, accompanied by a famine in its first year and a flood in its last year that intensified the misery.

The catastrophes of the seventeenth century were mere warm-ups for the eighteenth. In 1711 a great famine struck, lasting between five and seven years, during which people stopped measuring units of grain by the bag and started measuring by the handful. For the Western Sudan the century's worst catastrophe, indeed one of the worst ever to hit this part of the world, began in 1736 with a drought. When the rains finally came, they fell in torrents that washed away the crops. Two years later the bottom fell out of the ecosystem, and nature stopped producing for a year. The famine of 1738 killed half of the inhabitants of the Niger Bend. According to the *Tedzkiret en-Nisian*, people "covered their nudity with dried grasses," and the rich ate wild seeds and roots, food that only the most miserable would normally touch: "Men ate the cadavers of animals and human beings and coagulated blood in powder."

The government was paralyzed. Soldiers tried to ensure their own survival by exploiting civilians and warring among themselves. The famine generated an unspecified epidemic that was reinforced by a new dose of bubonic plague spreading south from Morocco. Trade was dislocated, the monetary system collapsed, and the economy was in chaos except where it was built on pillage. Hard times aggravated the enmity between peoples, greatly increasing the number of wars that raged across the land. Taken together, they comprised a sort of reverse Armageddon in which evil triumphed over good and the world did not come to a glorious end but lingered indefinitely in pain. Famine reinforced the slave economy as starving parents sold their children. Others migrated southward deep into the tropical forest. The disaster spread into the Sahara, where the population of some oases was wiped out, then moved on into North Africa. The city of Algiers shrunk to the size of a village, and the proud people of Morocco ate dogs when they could find them.

The impact of the disaster began to wane in 1744, although the drought lasted until 1756. The pest became endemic, reappearing from time to time. In 1755 an earthquake struck over a large area; it was interpreted as an omen that the travails were not over yet. An epidemic in 1758 was followed by a more severe one between 1762 and 1766. The survivors suffered still another famine in 1770–1771 and two kinds of plagues, bubonic in 1786–1796 and locusts in 1795–1796.

By the end of the eighteenth century the Western Sudan had lost most of its population, and its economic fabric was in tatters. If al-Mansur cannot be blamed for droughts, floods, or plagues, he did set in motion the events that radically altered the political structure in the interior of West Africa, creating a more predatory and less competent state that proved utterly incapable of responding to the vagaries of nature.

The End of the Sa'dis

Morocco's decline did not reach the nadir of that of the Western Sudan, nor did it drag on as long. But the government that Ahmad al-Mansur and his predecessors had so carefully constructed, indeed the dynasty itself, did not survive the fallout from his death. The Moroccan state paid a heavy price for its conquest of the Western Sudan. Its shock troops were the Andalusians and renegades the Sa'dis had depended on to hold Morocco together and keep their dynasty in power. Many of them were killed or died of disease, and how many survivors recrossed the Sahara remains uncertain. Al-Ifrani maintains that Mahmud Pasha, "after having established his authority solidly in these countries, sent back most of his troops to Morocco," and al-Zayyani claims that the sultan began rotating men out after three years. Al-Fishtali reports that the renegades were all withdrawn starting in 1599. However, in all accounts the pashas seem far more inclined to beg for reinforcements than to send veterans home. Zaydan once confided to Ahmad Baba that the Moroccans sent twenty-three thousand troops to the Western Sudan, of which barely five hundred ever returned.

In the decade after the death of al-Shaykh al-Ma'mun, Abd Allah and Zaydan turned away from each other. Abd Allah used Arab tribesmen as his military force, living more like a desert raider than a sultan. He died in October 1623 and was succeeded by a brother, Abd al-Malik al-Mu'tasim, described as "short of intelligence and young of age." This was the signal for total breakdown in the north. Arab tribesmen attacked Fez, and the city's quarters fought among themselves, their inhabitants raiding and plundering one another. The water supply was cut, barricades were set up, and women and children were charged tolls to walk in the streets.

In the south, Zaydan had his own problems. After al-Mansur, no one took Sa'di religious claims seriously. Militant marabouts came back with a vengeance, offering new messianic appeals and tapping into the inexhaustible well of religious enthusiasm. A new Mahdi named Ahmad Abu Mahalli appeared and defeated Zaydan in several battles, forcing him to abandon Marrakesh. The surviving ulama of Timbuktu hailed Abu Mahalli's conquest of Marrakesh as divine retribution for al-Mansur's crimes: Qadi Umar's curse had come true. Once installed in Marrakesh, Abu Mahalli added insult to injury by marrying Zaydan's mother and producing a son by her, whom he named Zaydan. In the meantime Zaydan found a champion, still another marabout named Yahya b. Abd Allah al-Hahi, who retook Marrakesh in October 1613, putting Abu Mahalli's head on the city's ramparts. Zaydan got his capital back, but he remained a puppet of al-Hahi until the latter died in 1626. Zaydan followed him a year later.

Thereafter, an assortment of religious leaders, adventurers, and tribal chiefs chipped away at what was left of the state that had been Morocco. Civil strife and political fragmentation were the order of the day. Political power became divided into so many competing entities that no one of them was capable of putting the country back together. All claimed to be dedicated to the same goal, the unity and stability of Morocco, but for fifty years their actions resulted in the same consequence, the disunity and instability of the country. The Sa'di army in the south degenerated into roving bands of gunmen barely distinguishable from bandits. In 1659 the last Sa'di sultan, Abu l'Abbas Ahmad IV, who controlled little more than Marrakesh, was murdered by a maternal uncle, thus ending the dynasty.

Requiem for a Dynasty

In the days of Abd al-Malik and Ahmad al-Mansur, Morocco appeared on the verge of joining the European international scene, if not as a principal, at least as an important secondary player. That possibility evaporated during the following half-century of chaos. Fortunately for Morocco, the seventeenth-century Mediterranean was a much more peaceful place than the sixteenth had been. But if the Spanish-Ottoman truce of 1580 made the western Mediterranean a safer neighborhood for a state like Morocco, it also proved fatal to Morocco's aspirations to become a power. As tensions in the western Mediterranean relaxed and Spain and the Ottoman Empire turned their interests in other directions, relations with Morocco became increasingly less important and finally entirely unimportant.

The larger world was changing. The Mediterranean basin, long the center of historical happenings, drifted into backwater status. Spain and the Ottoman Empire both turned a wrong corner and declined. The Turks had hammered themselves into exhaustion against Persia and were beginning to show a soft underbelly in the Balkans. They weren't going to conquer the world; they weren't even going to unite Islam any more than Spain would unite Christendom. Increasingly, Madrid's focus was on the New World, where Spain would enjoy a final century of glory before its imperial vitality was spent. Among European states, power was shifting northward. Few paid much attention as Morocco fell apart; they were busy slaughtering each other in the Thirty Years War, bent on determining once and for all whether God was a Protestant or a Catholic.

The frontier between North African Islam and Iberian Christianity ceased to be a hot spot. It slammed shut not just militarily and politically but culturally and economically. The Straits of Gibraltar came to separate not just two fortresses but two civilizations, both determined to prevent seepage from the other. The no man's land between them became the haunt of pirates who carried on private warfare. On the Moroccan side, the state that Muhammad al-Shaykh and Ahmad al-Mansur had built— a state that had pretensions to nation-statehood with a government that seemed to have been moving along the same highway of absolutism as France, Spain, and Russia—crumbled within decades. When the dust cleared, Morocco was again a country of cities, villages, tribes, *zawiyas*, and sometimes principalities, all moving in varying directions. Morocco may have missed an opportunity, but only if centralized, absolutist government is assumed to be better than government by autonomous local units. In any case, "what if history" is not history.

Political disintegration in Morocco was accompanied by social and cultural stagnation. The civil war ruined the cities, particularly Marrakesh, and urban civilization went into a downward spin from which it could not recover. All the major cities were inland: They pointed up into the mountains or out into the desert. They were not portals through which new influences easily flowed. Moroccan society remained so steeped in tradition, Moroccan culture so firmly conservative, that even the new concepts and ideas introduced by the Andalusians were largely ignored. The Moroccan ulama had always looked with concern on contacts between Moroccans and Europeans, and they disapproved of travel by their countrymen to lands outside Islam for fear they might be corrupted. After al-Mansur, Moroccans stopped going to Europe, and for the most part Europeans did not bother to go to Morocco.

Economic Morocco did not fare much better than political or cultural Morocco. Civil war and lawlessness disrupted sugar production in the Sus, and the English monopoly ended. Sugarcane cultivation shifted to Europe's plantation colonies, which in matters of climate and soil enjoyed considerable advantages over Morocco. Brazil and the islands of the Caribbean could produce mountains of sugar; Morocco could not compete. The Sus industry floundered, then disappeared. The English need for Moroccan saltpeter ended, too. The Moroccans no longer produced goods the Europeans wanted, and they had no money to buy what the Europeans sold. A cargo of Moroccan gold coins and jewelry dating from the 1630s was recently found off the coast of England, an indication that Morocco was being drained of its specie. As the Sa'dian state fragmented and the tax base shrank, the government attempted to compensate for lost income by increasing customs duties, thereby depressing the remaining trade.

By the eighteenth century the English, Dutch, and other Europeans did little direct trading with Morocco. Nor could Morocco join a bustling Islamic trade zone closer to home: Andalusia was gone, and the rest of North Africa was evolving under Turkish influence. Morocco was the terminus of a camel caravan commerce that had become largely irrelevant to world trade needs now that goods could go by ship much faster and cheaper than by camel. Morocco barely felt the ripples of change even as they became waves in the global economy. It became peripheral to the emerging Atlantic capitalist system in spite of the huge influx of gold and other loot that had once poured in. The rape of Songhay had no lasting effect except to ruin the Western Sudan. And if Morocco's economic and social institutions were not enhanced and no foundations were laid for commercial and industrial revolutions in the future, there were equally no fresh intellectual stimuli, no social upheavals, and no novel political forces to lead Morocco in new directions. To the outside world, Morocco went from being an important place on the map, a place of wealth and some power, a place to be reckoned with, to a place that had fallen apart, a place that might have been.

Epilogue

Ahmad al-Mansur did not turn out to be the true Mahdi, and there would be no universal caliphate based in Marrakesh. It is tempting to see him as a modern sort of fellow who knew this all along. In this line of thinking, religion, wealth, and reputation all served one purpose, that of power. This was the engine that drove him. But by using a religious pretext to justify what was obviously a naked grab for power, he lost the moral high ground among the religious establishment, an essential constituency of the Sa'di dynasty and a crucial element in the glue that held Morocco together. Ideology can serve a public relations function for only so long after its substance is gone; finally it just becomes a lie. Or at least that is the most common interpretation of Ahmad al-Mansur among historians outside Morocco. And if al-Mansur was not using religion in a very Machiavellian way, historians are even more bothered by what they perceive to be the disconnect between religion and morality—assuming, of course, that universal standards of morality exist.

Unfortunately, history never seems to lend itself to the simplest theory. If al-Mansur was ruthlessly practical in his pursuit of power, that does not eliminate the likelihood that he remained fancifully anachronistic in his goal of power. In other words, the disparity between his professed motives and the consequences of his actions should not necessarily cast doubt on those motives even if today, looking back, it seems obvious that the caliphate as a practical matter was an idea whose time had come and long gone. It was not going to work in the sixteenth century, and, in any case, Morocco could not have been the instrument to resurrect it. Al-Mansur's only major attempt to bring unity to the Islamic world, his conquest of the Songhay Empire, ultimately brought division and disunity to West Africa.

If Ahmad al-Mansur really did set out to reestablish the caliphate, and if he really did think he might be the Mahdi, and neither actually happened, it does not mean that from the beginning the caliphate and Mahdi ideas were only contrivances for mobilizing support from the simple or the dupable. One's life cannot be a complete fraud except in the eyes of others. Al-Mansur certainly thought God had singled him out to do great things: He was divinely chosen to carry out God's will. Doubtless he was ordained to be caliph; probably he was a little less certain about being Mahdi, but, in any case, God would guide him. Al-Mansur may have believed in this a little too much: If God intended that he unite the Muslim world, God would make this possible. The conquest of Songhay had been an obvious invitation. After that, al-Mansur must have thought, the rest of his destiny would become manifest in God's good time. That he might die before this happened probably never occurred to him.

Ahmad al-Mansur appears all too human, a man of vision and energy yet a very flawed man who refused to impose self-limits on his aspirations, his methods, or his goals. In the end his achievements were countered by his mistakes. He built an impressive structure, but much of it was made of sand. When he died, his edifice collapsed of its own weight. In the ledger of human suffering, the costs of his failures were enormous. But if his impact turned out to be more modest than his aspirations—if he didn't unify the Islamic world and prepare mankind for Judgment Day—this hardly casts him into the class of historical do-nothings. His real legacy, for better or worse, was more concrete and focused. His imprint on his own time can best be seen through his contemporaries. The Ottoman Sultan, the King of Spain, and the Queen of England all took him seriously. Unimportant or irrelevant states and their rulers are left out of big power stratagems: They are ignored or told what to do. But not

Morocco under Ahmad al-Mansur. What was considered one of the most stunning achievements of the day, the conquest and looting of Songhay, was entirely his doing. And if Morocco did not make events of quite that magnitude happen in the Mediterranean, the government in Marrakesh was an important party to major events there.

Outside Morocco, al-Mansur is still remembered primarily for his invasion of the Western Sudan and the dreadful consequences that ensued. He and his henchmen, Judar Pasha and Mahmud Pasha, occupy a deserved corner in West Africa's rogues' gallery. West Africa, however, had a revenge of sorts. Al-Mansur thought the Songhay Empire would open the door to world conquest; instead it proved to be a cul-de-sac in which Morocco was condemned to wander until its energies were exhausted. Morocco never recovered from its victory over Songhay; it proved to be the ultimate lose-lose situation.

Al-Mansur's record for Morocco is more equivocal, although here critics are often so busy pointing out what he didn't do that they miss even his more obvious accomplishments. Al-Mansur inherited many of his problems; his error was that he made no determined effort to fix them. He never attempted, for example, to redress the contradiction passed down from his father, Muhammad al-Shaykh, in reconciling Sa'dian ideology with the practicalities of Sa'dian geopolitics or trade policies. A more immediate problem was the system of succession, said to go back to the wishes of his grandfather, Muhammad al-Qa'im. If al-Mansur took advantage of Songhay weakness caused in part by a flawed system of succession, he failed to see the consequences of his own actions, or inactions, thereby condemning his dynasty to the same dustbin as the Askiyas. A more difficult problem to fix, and one al-Mansur addressed more persistently if no more successfully, was that of money. The Sa'dis had always had a problem with income versus expenditures; under al-Mansur this problem became an enigma. He was the beneficiary of two bountiful windfalls, yet he could not develop an indigenous source of wealth sufficient to establish and sustain a state apparatus.

Ahmad al-Mansur was a remarkable man, a catalyst for his time, a maker of events whose achievements were built on other remarkable men, his father and brothers. He is often hailed as the family's great visionary, the nation-builder. His problem, according to this line of thinking, was that he was too far ahead of his time. Perhaps. But it is fair to ask what kind of vision he really had. To attribute to him the foresight of seeing the state of Morocco in its modern form would be to elevate him far above contemporary monarchs in western Europe who ruled over countries much farther along in this process. Like them, his focus was, more properly speaking, dynastic rather than national, and when given the opportunity his true interests turned out to be imperial. And if he did conceive of Morocco as a national polity, he still had to impose his state on Moroccan society rather than nurture its growth from that society. Always he had to rely too much on brute force and too little on organically rooted institutions. In his defense he did not have time to foster a national growth of one from the other, but the gap between them was never filled. He left Morocco much as he had found it, a society of autonomous units.

Al-Mansur also left Morocco an independent state, no small achievement considering the dangers and difficulties of his time. In the sixteenth century the Hapsburgs were collecting states, and the Ottomans were consuming them: Morocco stood between the two. Some critics believe the failed policies of al-Mansur and his dynasty condemned Morocco to fall to European imperialism. True, Morocco fell, but that happened two and a half centuries later. Practically all the rest of Africa, including all of North Africa, fell as well, and Morocco was the last to go. It was also among the first to liberate itself, after only forty-five years.

If the Sa'dis who succeeded Ahmad al-Mansur disgraced themselves, they did not discredit the ideal of the Prophet's family as a source of political legitimacy. When Morocco finally came back together in the late seventeenth century, it did so under a new dynasty, the Alawis, another family of *shurafa*. Like the Sa'dis, the Alawis were able to cut across the kinship and tribal structures that kept Morocco apart. And over the ensuing centuries, the Alawis produced a number of powerful and effective sultans. But no attempt was made to bring Morocco down the road of centralization, national consciousness, or, for a long time, modern nation-state building. Perhaps that is why the Alawi dynasty survived.

That the institution of monarchy has survived in Morocco says much for the rulers of its dynasties. Over the centuries the sharifian monarchy has represented order and stability; it has tied people, state, and faith into one domain. Even today, when the remnants of monarchy around the world are largely relegated to ceremony, the kings of Morocco play an active role in the governance of their nation.

Unfortunately, the early Alawi sultans felt themselves to be living in the shadow of their predecessors. The Sa'di claim to true shurafahood was called into question. They were, it was said, descended from the tribe of Muhammad's wet nurse rather than from the Prophet himself. The greatest of the early Alawi sultans, Mawlay Ismail, felt so intimidated by the greatest of the Sa'di sultans that he committed an act of unforgivable desecration to exorcise the ghost of Ahmad al-Mansur from the Moroccan body politic. Al-Mansur had built al-Badi as a monument to his glory to last throughout time like the great pyramids. In 1711 Mawlay Ismail ordered it torn down and its marble carried off to be used in palaces elsewhere. Today its sprawling ruins are a popular stop for tourist buses cruising the sights of Marrakesh.

A Note on the Sources

Primary Sources

Serious scholarly research on Ahmad al-Mansur and the Sa'di dynasty will lead to the massive work by Henry de Castries, Pierre de Cenival, Robert Ricard, Chantal de la Véronne, and Philipp de Cosse Brissac (eds.), *Sources inédit de l'histoire de Maroc*, première série, Dynastie saadienne (1530–1660), Paris: Leroux-Geuthner, 1905–1972. Of particular interest will be *Archives et bibliothèques de Portugal*, 5 vols.; *Archives et bibliothèques d' Espagne*, 3 vols.; and *Archives et bibliothèques d' Angleterre*, 5 vols.

Of sources more readily available, the American student should begin with Mohammed Essenghir Ben Elhadj Ben Abdallah Eloufrani (al-Ifrani), *Nozhet-Elhâdi: Histoire de la Dynastie Saadienne au Maroc (1511–1670)*, O. Houdas (ed. and tr.), Paris: Ernest Leroux, 1889. Portions of al-Ifrani are translated into English in a rather peculiar book, T. H. Weir, *The Shaikhs of Morocco in the XVIth Century*, London: George A. Morton, 1904. Weir weaves long passages from al-Ifrani within a work of hagiography by Ibn Askar, a scholar who died fighting for al-Mutawakkil at Wadi al-Makhazin. Al-Ifrani's sections from Abd al-Aziz al-Fishtali, *Manahil al-Safa*, are taken from only one volume, and scholars today wonder whether al-Fishtali's work ever amounted to the reported eight volumes. The most complete version now available (in Arabic) was published in 1974 by Abd al-Krim Kurayyim.

As a balance to al-Ifrani and al-Fishtali, see *Extraits Inédits Relatifs au Maghreb (Géographie et Histoire)*, Edward Fagnan (tr.), Alger: Jules Carbonel, 1924, 360–457, "Sur la dynastie Sa'dienne," which contains the work by the Anonymous

Chronicler of Fez. Fagnan's work also contains, in French translation, a fragment of Mustafa al-Jannabi's *Al-Bahr al-Zakhar*
that concerns the Sa'dis and other Moroccan dynasties; see
285–359. Roger Le Tourneau, "Histoire de la Dynastie Sa'adide,"
Revue de l'Occident musulman et de la Méditerranée, 23 (1977),
1–107, provides a translation of the Sa'di section of Abu al-Qasim
al-Zayyani, *Al-Tarjuman al-Mu'rib 'an duwal al-Mashriq wa
al-Maghrib*.

Other important primary or contemporary sources include the
account of António de Saldanha, in António Dias Farinha (ed.),
*Crónica de Almançor, Sultão de Marrocos (1578–1603), de
António de Saldanha*, Lisbon: Instituto de Investigação Cientifica
Tropical, 1997. A modern French translation is provided. The
work of Leo Africanus together with commentary by John Pory
can be found in *The History and Description of Africa and of
the Notable Things Therein Contained*, New York: Burt Franklin,
1963, 3 vols. (originally published by the Hakluyt Society in
1600). The best description of the Battle of Wadi al-Makhazin
is attributed to an Italian although there is speculation that the
real author was someone else; the Spanish ambassador to Lisbon
has been suggested. It is available in English translation; see
Franchi Conestaggio, *The Historie of the Uniting of the Kingdom
of Portugall to the Crowne of Castil*, London, 1600.

Sources on the Songhay Empire and the Moroccans in the
Western Sudan must begin with John O. Hunwick, *Timbuktu
and the Songhay Empire*, Leiden: Brill, 1999. Hunwick provides the only substantial English translation of a Sudanese
Chronicle, Abd al-Rahman al-Sadi's *Tarikh al-Sudan* although
only up to 1613 (the original goes up to 1655–1656). A French
translation by O. Houdas published in 1913–1914 was
reprinted in 1964. Material quoted from al-Sadi in the preceding text is taken from both the Houdas and Hunwick editions.
Hunwick's book also includes a section from al-Ifrani's work
that concerns the conquest of Songhay as well as the account of
the Anonymous Spaniard and some letters written by al-Mansur,
from which I have taken citations. The section in al-Sadi relating to the Moroccan conquest can also be found in English
translation in Robert O. Collins, *African History: Text and
Readings*, vol. I, *West African History*, New York: Marcus

Wiener Publisher, 1990. Mahmud Kati, *Tarikh al-Fattach*, O. Houdas (ed. and tr.) and M. Delafosse (tr.), Paris: Adrien-Maisonneuve, 1913–1914 (reprinted 1964), is still available only in French, as is the major work on the later period of the pashalik, the anonymous biographical dictionary, *Tedzkiret an-Nisian fi Akhbar Molouk es-Soudan*, O. Houdas (tr.), Paris: Adrien Maisonneuve, 1966.

Secondary Sources

Ahmad al-Mansur and the Sa'di dynasty are favorite topics of Moroccan historians; unfortunately, most of their work has been done in Arabic, with smaller amounts in French. Works on related topics like King Sebastian of Portugal or the Morisco-Andalusian tragedy are available mostly in Portuguese or Spanish, although a reasonably sympathetic treatment of Sebastian in English, for example, can be found in Marjorie Bowen, *Sundry Great Gentlemen: Some Essays in Historical Biography*, New York: Dodd, Mead and Company, 1928, 117–168, and a thorough account of the Morisco-Andalusians is now available in L.P. Harvey, *Muslims in Spain, 1500 to 1614*, Chicago: University of Chicago Press, 2005. This following discussion considers only works in English.

To provide a general background for viewing Morocco in the larger context of North African history, see Jamel M. Abun-Nasr, *A History of the Maghrib in the Islamic Period*, Cambridge: Cambridge University Press, 1987; Abdallah Laroui, *The History of the Maghrib: An Interpretive Essay*, Princeton: Princeton University Press, 1977; and M. el Fasi, "Morocco," in *General History of Africa*, V, B. A. Ogot (ed.), Berkeley: University of California Press, 1992, 200–232. For a broader perspective on the history of the Islamic world, students may consult Ira Lapidus, *A History of Islamic Societies*, Cambridge: Cambridge University Press, 1988.

The only complete work in English on Ahmad al-Mansur's reign is a doctoral dissertation by Stephen Charles Cory, "Chosen by God to Rule: The Caliphate and Political Legitimacy in Early Modern Morocco," University of California–Santa Barbara, 2002. This is an extremely useful study on al-Mansur's attempt at resurrecting the caliphate, and it includes much else of interest. A more focused discussion can be found in M. E. Combs-Schilling, *Sacred Performances: Islam, Sexuality, and Sacrifice*, New York: Columbia University Press, 1989, which examines al-Mansur's use of ritual, particularly in the celebration of the Prophet's birthday. A distilled version of Combs-Schilling's thesis is available, along with related topics, in Rahma Bourqia and Susan Gilson Miller (eds.), *In the Shadow of the Sultan: Culture, Power, and Politics in Morocco*, Cambridge, Massachusetts: Harvard University Press, 1999.

For background on the religious atmosphere in Morocco leading into the Sa'di period and particularly on al-Jazuli and his movement, Vincent J. Cornell, *Realm of the Saint: Power and Authority in Moroccan Sufism*, Austin: University of Texas Press, 1998, can be consulted. A concise examination of Sa'di use of religious themes is available in Daniel Pipes, "The Rise of the Sa'dis in Morocco," *The Maghreb Review*, 9 (1984), 46–52. Henry Munson, Jr., *Religion and Power in Morocco*, New Haven: Yale University Press, 1993, provides a good look at *shurafa*, ulama, *qutbs*, Sufism, *baraka*, *fatwas*, and similar subjects as they relate to the Moroccan monarchy.

The best examination of al-Mansur's Mahdist pretensions and the millennialist atmosphere of his time can be found in two articles by John Ralph Willis: "Morocco and the Western Sudan, Fin de Siècle–Fin de Temps, Some Aspects of Religion and Culture to 1600," *The Maghreb Review*, 14 (1989), 91–96; and "The Bay'a in Islam and Some Aspects of the Bay'a in Morocco's Relations with the Western Sudan," in *Le Maroc et l'Afrique Subsaharienne aux Débuts des Temps Modernes: Les Sa'diens et l'Empire Songhay*, Institut des Études Africaines, Université Mohammed V, Rabat, Maroc (ed.), Casablanca: Laboratoire Informatique de l'I.E.A., 1995, 219–235. This collection contains papers presented at a colloquium by an international panel of scholars, mostly in French and Arabic but some in English. Of particular interest among the latter are Dahiru Yahia, "The Ideological Framework of Sa'di Foreign Policy," 237–249; and E. Ann McDougall, "The Question of Tegaza and the Conquest of Songhay: Some Saharan Considerations," 251–272.

The rise of Sa'di power in Morocco, with emphasis on state building and the impact of the gunpowder revolution, is examined in a well-researched and thorough study by Weston F. Cook, Jr., *The Hundred Years War for Morocco: Gunpowder and the Military Revolution in the Early Modern Muslim World*, Boulder: Westview Press, 1994. The complicated geopolitical world of the sixteenth century and Morocco's place in it are well analyzed by Andrew C. Hess, *The Forgotten Frontier: A History of the Sixteenth Century Ibero-African Frontier*, Chicago: University of Chicago Press, 1978, and Dahiru Yahya, *Morocco in the Sixteenth Century: Problems and Patterns in African Foreign Policy*, Atlantic Highlands, NJ: Humanities Press, 1981. More focused studies of interest include: for the Ottoman Empire, Michael Brett, "Morocco and the Ottomans: The Sixteenth Century in North Africa," *Journal of African History*, 25 (1984), 331–341, and Abderrahmane El Moudden, "The Idea of the Caliphate between Moroccans and Ottomans: Political and Symbolic stakes in the 16th and 17th Century Maghrib," *Studia Islamica*, 82 (1995), 103–112; for Spain, Amira K. Bennison, "Liminal States: Morocco and the Iberian Frontier between the Twelfth and Nineteenth Centuries," in Julia Clancy-Smith, *North African Islam and the Mediterranean World: From the Almoravids to the Algerian War*, London: Frank Cass, 2001, 11–28; and for Bornu, B. G. Martin, "Mai Idris of Bornu and the Ottoman Turks, 1576–1578," *International Journal of Middle Eastern Studies*, 3 (1972), 470–490.

The Portuguese invasion of 1578 is described at length in E. W. Bovill, *The Battle of Alcazar: An Account of the Defeat of Don Sebastian of Portugal at El-Ksar el Kebir*, London: Batchworth Press, 1952. This author is better known for a widely used, although now dated, examination of the trans-Saharan trade that tied Morocco to the Western Sudan, *The Golden Trade of the Moors*, 2nd ed., London: Oxford University Press, 1968 (reprinted by Markus Wiener, 1995). An assessment based on more recent research of this topic can be found in Richard L. Smith, "Medieval Coins, West African Gold: Secrets and Lies Behind the Trans-Saharan Trade," *The Celator, Journal of Ancient and Medieval Coinage*, Part I, 18 (Oct. 2004), 6–21, and Part II, 18 (Nov. 2004), 20–28.

As a character in world history Ahmad al-Mansur is best re-membered (or vilified) for sending Judar's army to destroy the Songhay Empire. Aspects of the Moroccan invasion are explored by Lansine Kaba, "Archers, Musketeers, and Mosquitoes: The Moroccan Invasion of the Sudan and the Songhay Resistance (1591–1612)," *Journal of African History*, 22 (1981), 457–475; and J. O. Hunwick, "Ahmad Baba and the Moroccan Invasion of the Sudan (1591)," *Journal of the Historical Society of Nigeria*, 2 (1962), 311–326. An assessment of the overall impact can be found in M. Abitbol, "The End of the Songhay Empire," in *General History of Africa*, V, B. A. Ogot (ed.), Berkeley: University of California Press, 1992, 300–326. The disintegra-tion of the Sa'di state is analyzed in B. A. Mojuetan, "Legitimacy in a Power State: Moroccan Politics in the Seventeenth Century During the Interregnum," *International Journal of Middle East Studies*, 13 (1981), 347–360.

Glossary

Abbasid From Abbas, uncle of Muhammad; second caliphal dynasty, which ruled from Baghdad, 749–1258; later served as puppets to the rulers in Cairo until 1517.

abd "Servant of"; used in conjunction with one of the ninety-nine names of God, as in Abd Allah or Abd al-Malik.

Alawi From Ali, son-in-law of Muhammad; dynasty that succeeded the Sa'dis and continues on the throne of Morocco today.

Almohad Second great empire centered in Morocco, 1147–1269; also referred to as al-Muwahhidun.

amir (emir) Originally, a military commander and by extension a prince or governor; Amir al-Muminin (Commander of the Faithful) was a caliphal title.

Andalusians Refugees from al-Andalus, Muslim Spain, many of whom settled in Morocco; comprised elite units in the Moroccan army.

Arma From Arabic *al-rumat*, "shooter"; descendants of the Moroccan army in the Western Sudan who comprised a ruling military caste to c. 1800.

arquebus Matchlock shoulder gun common in the sixteenth century; shot by an arquebusier.

Askiya Ruling dynasty of the Songhay Empire, 1492–1591; also used as a title signifying "emperor."

Avis Ruling dynasty of Portugal, 1385–1580; the death of Sebastian I signaled its end.

al-Badi "The Marvelous" or "the Incomparable"; a magnificent palace in Marrakesh constructed by Ahmad al-Mansur; destroyed under the succeeding dynasty.

Balama Commander of Songhay troops in the west; in 1588 the Balama Muhammad al-Sadiq led a major but unsuccessful revolt.

baraka "Blessedness"; spiritual power possessed by a holy person; can be transmitted.

bayʻa Oath of allegiance given by a Muslim to his political leader.

Berbers Indigenous (pre-Arab) inhabitants of North Africa.

caliph (khalifa) Successor of Muhammad as head of all Muslims; also used to signify a deputy or representative appointed to serve over a particular region.

caracole Maneuver in which mounted gunmen charged an enemy in waves, firing a round, then retreating to reload.

casbah (qasba) Fortress.

al-Dajjal "The Deceiver"; the Antichrist who will appear before the end of the world to corrupt many; will be killed by Jesus, perhaps with help from the Mahdi.

diwan Used in the Ottoman regencies of North Africa and adopted for use in Morocco; council of advisers serving as a ruler's cabinet.

eunuch Castrated man, often a highly placed slave of a ruler.

fatwa Ruling on a point of Islamic law issued by a mufti.

Fezi (Fasi) Inhabitant of the city of Fez.

Granada Last independent Muslim state of al-Andalus on the Iberian Peninsula; conquered by Christian Spain (Castile and Aragon) in 1492.

hadith Sayings of the Prophet Muhammad or reports of his deeds; considered second only to the Qur'an as a source of authority for Muslims.

hijra (hegira) "Abandonment" or "emigration"; refers to the Prophet Muhammad's flight from Mecca to Medina in 622 C.E., which marks the beginning of the Muslim calendar, designated A.H.

Hi-koy Songhay title, "Chief of the Boats"; admiral of the riverain navy and highest ranking officer in the Songhay military.

imam "He who stands in front"; usually refers to the prayer leader in a mosque; can also be used by a caliph to signify leadership over all Islam.

Jazuliyya Sufi order founded by Muhammad al-Jazuli in the fifteenth century; it stressed veneration of the Prophet and his family.

jihad "Struggle"; commonly used to designate a holy war against unbelievers.

Kapudan Pasha Supreme admiral of the Ottoman Empire.

Mahdi "Rightly Guided One"; a messianic leader sent to guide Muslims as the end of the world approaches.

marabout French corruption of *murabit*, now commonly used; refers to a holy man, one who possesses *baraka*.

Mawlid ʿId al-Mawlid, the celebration of the Prophet Muhammad's birthday.

Mina (Costa da Mina) Literally, "Mine"; refers to a stretch of coastline in modern Ghana noted for its trade in gold.

mithqal Unit of weight in the Islamic world, usually 4.25 grams; used to measure gold dust.

Moriscos Hispano-Muslims officially declared to be Christians after 1502; in exile they became known as Andalusians.

Moor From *Maurus*, Latin reference to an inhabitant of ancient Mauretania; a term Europeans applied to the peoples of western North Africa of mixed Berber-Arab culture.

mufti High Muslim legal scholar who delivered authoritative but nonbinding opinions on Islamic law (fatwas).

pasha (bashaw) Military commander or provincial governor in Ottoman North Africa; adopted by the Moroccan army.

qadi Judge of Qurʾanic law; often assumed the role of leader of the ulama in an Islamic community.

qaʾid Military title, roughly, "Commander"; a rank below pasha used in Morocco and Ottoman North Africa.

Qurʾan (Koran) Holy book of Islam, transmitted from God to the Prophet Muhammad.

Quraysh Powerful Arabian tribe of which the Prophet Muhammad was a member.

qutb "Pole"; a Sufi term referring to the axial saint of a period whose virtue and piety made him an exemplar for other Muslims.

Reconquista Spanish reference to wars between Christians and Muslims on the Iberian peninsula that ended with the fall of Granada in 1492.

renegade (uluj) From Spanish *renegare*, "to deny"; a Christian who has converted to Islam; prominent in the Moroccan military.

Sa'di Sharifian family with roots in the Dar'a Valley; ruling dynasty of Morocco 1549–1659.

sharif (pl. *shurafa*) "Noble"; usually refers to a descendant of the Prophet Muhammad.

shaykh (pl. shuyukh) From Arabic signifying elder or venerable old man; a form of respectful address applied to a chief or communal leader.

Songhay (Songhai) Nilo-Saharan-speaking people who inhabit the Niger Valley and its environs from Timbuktu east and south to Dendi; established a great empire in the late fifteenth and sixteenth centuries.

spahi From Persian *sipah*, "armed"; Ottoman and later Moroccan cavalryman whose primary weapon was a gun.

Sufism Islamic mysticism in which the goal is personal communion with God; in North Africa Sufis were usually organized into brotherhoods.

sultan Temporal ruler of an Islamic country; title assumed by an emperor or very powerful king.

Sunna Elite infantry corps of slave soldiers in the Songhay army.

Taghaza Salt mine in the central Sahara; principal producer of salt for West Africa until the seventeenth century.

Taoudeni (Tawdani) Salt mine in the central Sahara, south of Taghaza, that assumed the role of principal producer after Taghaza.

Tuwat (Tuat) Oasis region in the central Sahara; it served as a major resting place or "refreshment station" for trans-Saharan caravans.

Tuaregs Berber people of the Sahara, conspicuous because the men but not the women wore veils; noted herdsmen and camel breeders, they enjoyed a reputation for prowess in battle.

ulama (sing. alim) "Men of knowledge"; a corporate body of scholars and religious functionaries in an Islamic city sometimes serving as a ruling oligarchy, as in Timbuktu.

wadi (oued) River, often seasonal.

Wangara (Juula) Mythical Land of Gold believed to lie deep in the West African interior; actually a class of Sudanese merchants who traded gold and other products.

Wattasid Dynasty preceding the Sa'di as rulers of Morocco.

Western Sudan From Arabic *Sūdān*, "black," hence "Land of the Blacks"; region of mostly grassland south of the Sahara and north of the tropical forest stretching from the Senegal Valley to Lake Chad.

zawiya "Corner"; the lodge of a Sufist brotherhood often built in proximity to the tomb of a saint.

Index